the JOY of Scrapbooking

Sara McMartin

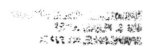

*Scrapbooking has taught me to cherish simple, everyday moments
with my children. I notice and document things that would normally slip
by me if they didn't have to pass through my 'scrapbooker's filter.'
Most people don't take pictures of their kids' shoes, their favorite snacks, or the
contents of their messy backpacks—but I do because it helps me remember
each and every unique stage that we pass through as they grow older.*

Cathy Goins, scrapbooker

the JOY of Scrapbooking

Kerry Arquette

Andrea Zocchi

& Darlene D'Agostino

cantata books

LARK
BOOKS
A Division of
Sterling Publishing Co., Inc.
New York

Executive Editor
Kerry Arquette

Editor
Darlene D'Agostino

Art Director/Designer
Andrea Zocchi

Cover Design
Andrea Zocchi

Designer
Susha Roberts

Contributing Writer
Lois Duncan

Copy Editor
Dena Twinem

Created and produced
by Cantata Books Inc.

P.O. Box 740040
Arvada, CO 80006-0040

www.cantatabooks.com

Library of Congress Cataloging-in-Publication Data

Arquette, Kerry.

The joy of scrapbooking / Kerry Arquette, Andrea Zocchi, Darlene

D'Agostino.

p. cm.

Includes index.

ISBN 1-57990-763-6 (hardcover)

1. Photograph albums. 2. Scrapbooks. 3. Photographs–Conservation and

restoration. I. Zocchi, Andrea. II. D'Agostino, Darlene. III. Title.

TR501.A7645 2006

745.593–dc22

2006007342

10 9 8 7 6 5 4 3 2

Published by Lark Books, A Division of
Sterling Publishing Co., Inc.
387 Park Avenue South, New York, N.Y. 10016

© 2006 Cantata Books Inc.

Distributed in Canada by Sterling Publishing, c/o Canadian Manda Group,
165 Dufferin Street, Toronto, Ontario, Canada M6K 3H6

Distributed in the United Kingdom by GMC Distribution Services,
Castle Place, 166 High Street, Lewes, East Sussex, England BN7 1XU

Distributed in Australia by Capricorn Link (Australia) Pty Ltd.,
P.O. Box 704, Windsor, NSW 2756 Australia

The written instructions, photographs, designs, patterns, and projects in this volume are intended for the personal use of the reader and may be reproduced for that purpose only. Any other use, especially commercial use, is forbidden under law without written permission of the copyright holder.

Every effort has been made to ensure that all the information in this book is accurate. However, due to differing conditions, tools, and individual skills, the publisher cannot be responsible for any injuries, losses, and other damages that may result from the use of the information in this book.

If you have questions or comments about this book, please contact:
Lark Books, 67 Broadway, Asheville, NC 28801. Tel: (828) 253-0467

Manufactured in China

ISBN 13: 978-1-57990-763-1

ISBN 10: 1-57990-763-6

For information about custom editions, special sales, premium and corporate purchases, please contact Sterling Special Sales Department at 800-805-5489 or special-sales@sterlingpub.com.

Dedication: A project this expansive requires effort and input from an army of dedicated people. We are very lucky to have had so many across the world willing to share their expertise, time and talent. This book is the love child of editors, writers, poets, artists, models, designers and photographers. It grew from concept to reality, nurtured by their creativity. Roll out the red carpet because we'd like to thank...

Our talented co-author and editor, Darlene D'Agostino. She put up with our craziness and contributed a dollop of her own, which made working on this book together a kick and a half. We'd also like to acknowledge our remarkable editors at Lark Publishing, Carol Taylor and Deborah Morgenthal, whose deft minds helped mold the project and whose faith in us allowed us to *"do our thang."*

(Andrea to Kerry: "You can't say 'thang' in a dedication. People will think that you can't spell!")
(Kerry to Andrea: "It's called 'creative license'. I kan right 'thang' if I whant.")

We'd like to thank Todd Kaderabek, who guides Lark's Production Department and Chris Bryant, who heads Lark's Design Department. They are very cool guys who know their tha—
(Andrea to Kerry: "—If you are going to insist on writing like that, I'm going to take over!")

(This is Andrea writing) We'd also like to thank our families, beginning with my wife, Joann, for contributing her photographic gifts to the project and for shouldering most of the parenting responsibilities while I worked; my brother Steve for good advice; and my sister-in-law Debby for her support. I'd also like to thank my sons, Marco and Luca, for modeling when they would much rather have been outside jumping on the tramp. *(Kerry to Andrea: "I think you need to say 'trampoline' or readers will think that Marco and Luca are abusing a hobo. BTW, it's my turn...")*

(This is Kerry writing) Thanks to my incredible kids, Erin, Brittin and Ryan, who have *(almost)* uncomplainingly put up with takeout meals and limited amounts of clean laundry while I worked. And thanks to Danita Koehler for stepping into my empty "Mommy shoes" when needed. I'm also grateful to my mother, Lois Duncan, for contributing her writing gifts; and my father, Donald Arquette, for his unfailing support; Mark, for his belief in me; my sister, Robin, for listening to me gripe; and my...

(Andrea to Kerry: "We only have a page for this dedication and we're running out of room! We still need to thank...")

Those talented artists whose work graces these pages, and to scrapbookers around the world who are dedicated to the artful preservation of personal memories. Their time and talent preserve stories that will echo across generations to come.

(Kerry to Andrea: "Did we remember everybody?") (Andrea to Kerry: "I thang so...")

Table of Contents

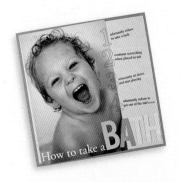

Understand the Mechanics of Successful Design

Relish the Craft

Table of Contents

Discover the Joy of Scrapbooking

Embrace this appreciation of life

Tick. That second is past, forever chased by those that follow. Like a tributary, they flow into history, blending with the minutes, days and years that went before. As the singular seconds become part of a greater whole, that moment, that single moment, is easily forgotten. Yet in the life of a scrapbooker, that moment will not be taken for granted.

To a scrapbooker, each day is a new canvas. Camera-ready with a heightened sense of awareness of life's important moments, she revels in her toddler's sticky ice-cream-mustached kisses, the robust smell of Sunday morning coffee, the soft lavenders and vibrant yellows of a blooming iris. Completed scrapbook pages elicit a range of emotions. They recall individual events, but also document personal journeys and growth. They are proof that life has been lived to its fullest.

While scrapbooks ultimately serve as legacies for future generations, modern scrapbookers reap the benefits of the craft here and now. In the process of creating the pages within an album, scrapbookers stretch and grow. They learn to express love, to tell their own story, to connect with the future and to surrender to their creative muse.

Life is fleeting. Children grow up. Loved ones pass on. But time stands still in a scrapbook. And the joy of creating a scrapbook changes the artist forever.

Wendy Gibson

" *Joy delights in joy.* "

Shakespeare

Express Your Love

Scrapbook pages should throb with emotion and ring with sincerity, showing others that you care

KALEB

AGE 10

2004

you dream. believe. do. be you.

Samuel Cole

You Dream. Believe. Do. Be You.

The inner and outer beauty of a boy is captured on this sterling scrapbook page. The page, created by the model's uncle, includes a journaled tag on which the artist shares his love for and pride in his nephew.

As you grow and become...always remember you are loved and so very special.
Samuel Cole

"I love you." While a scrapbook cannot replace the need a child has to hear those words, it can underscore the message. A 2-year-old who sees her first toddling steps featured in a photo on a scrapbook page becomes aware of her parent's pride in her accomplishment. And a 4-year-old who sits on her mother's lap and admires pages detailing her first spoken words enjoys the closeness of the snuggle-moment and the understanding that her parent is listening to her thoughts.

In the years that follow, that child's life is filled with events large and small. Her parent records them with photos and journaling—the first day of school, that first soccer goal, middle-school jitters, high-school prom and graduation. The pages are testimony to the fact that her parents valued her accomplishments and cherished both her and the times they shared.

When she's grown, the scrapbooks she inherits will remind her of her journey and those who traveled by her side. She will be able to actually hold a symbol of her parent's love and devotion in her hands.

Lisa VanderVeen

Tell Your Story

Scrapbook journaling encourages you to explore and reveal your innermost thoughts and feelings

Journaling on a scrapbook page is often as important as the photos. When words accompany images, others who read them experience the feelings behind the photos. If scrapbook pages include names, dates and locations, images are placed into a historical context.

Everyone has a story that begs to be told. In fact, you have many. As a scrapbooker, you are in the unique position to document not only your own story, but the stories of those you love. The stories may be slices of life, or span years. You may tell them with a sprinkling of words, or choose to elaborate on the details.

Journaling may help open the floodgates to emotions and lead to reflection and the processing of the complexities of life. Journal with abandon, setting aside self-criticism about your writing talents. This is your story, your art and your moment to share it.

Heidi Schueller

> *The three little people that once wore these slightly dirty old shoes now fit into double digits. And I'm left yearning for those little sneakers to be filled once again. Thoughts of another heartbeat ticking inside me makes me smile and I want so much to prevent these shoes from becoming part of history...But, I must look toward the future. Three sets of feet are more than enough to feed, clothe and shelter. There is no time for four, no money for four, no energy for four and no vacancy for four...Yet there is enough love for four and these shoes.*

Three or Four

Sometimes there is no better forum to express strong emotion than on a scrapbook page. The sunbathed baby shoes on this page are symbolic of a mother's acceptance that she will have no more babies on which to put them.

7am...You crawl into my bed and whisper...as a statement...not a question, 'Mom, you love me forever and ever and always and always, huh.'

Even when you tell me you hate me, or you tell me you love me, or when I am disappointed in your behavior, or when you fill me with pride, or when you hit your sister or tell her you love her, or when you embarrass me or make a great first impression, always and always, forever and ever, I love you! It's an 'I love you' out of the blue—and no longer considered a precursor to finding a bag of sugar dragged through the house. It's the caress of your leg whilst driving with the occasional prompt of, 'Mommy, love on my leg.' It's letters in your mailbox and in the pictures you draw for us. It's our nightly prayers. It's what you tell your little sis and what we are teaching her. It's sweet snuggles and big bear hugs. It's a ton of kisses. It was your first sentence you wrote. It's the whisper of sweet dreams in your ear whilst you sleep. It's the sacrifices and in the sorry's. It's in these pages. It's the foundation of our family, it is unconditional, always present, always felt, always expressed, forever known, forever constant, forever here... aka I love you!

Tracy Austin

Love Forever and Always

A child needs to do nothing in order to be loved by her mother, and there is truly nothing she can do to stop that love. The journaling on this tender page details that sentiment. The journaling, handwritten with a marker, flows around the photo and is embellished with charms, stickers, rub-ons, ribbon and a wide variety of other decorative touches.

Tracy Austin

SHARING STORIES IN A SCRAPBOOK

Every person, every event, every moment has a story. Scrapbook pages can share stories that...

...document family history.
...record the beauty of a season.
...blend a new family.
...pass down values and beliefs.
...prove happy times do and can exist again.

...celebrate milestones and achievements.
...help heal after a challenge or loss.
...remind oneself of favorite things.
...introduce a vivid personality.
...keep traditions alive.

Connect the Past and Future

Scrapbooking compels you to explore and share family history, linking generations and throwing a light on familial similarities and differences

As a scrapbooker, you are a historian. Through your labors of love you create books that house an unprecedented wealth of genealogical information. With these albums in hand, future generations will have a better idea of where they have come from, which may enable them to more easily determine where they are headed.

You, the scrapbooker, are a journalist. Like news reporters, you research the facts, provide human-interest accounts of happenings, put the pieces together and create a comprehensive, cohesive account of an event. With photos and words, you archive "today" so that it can be better understood "tomorrow."

> *By preserving these memories in a scrapbook, my children can look at them again and again over the years, each time relating to a different aspect of the experience.*
> Debra Marsh

Okinawa

The combination of rich historical detail and personal anecdotes on the pages above and on the right provide significant information about a major event in this family's history. The artist researched the Battle of Okinawa and interviewed her in-laws for the documentary-style pages that include fold-out elements rich with photographic and written detail.

Debra Marsh

Tool Time 1898

A photo of the artist's grandfather and grand uncle that was taken to advertise their hardware store is the focal point of this terrific heritage page. An original song, written by her grand uncle, is also featured on the page. Patterned paper, stickers and a grouping of aged embellishments work perfectly to support the memorabilia.

Carolyn Cleveland

PRESERVING YOUR HISTORY

What you scrapbook today will be significant tomorrow. Scrapbook about the following:

Material Items: What objects can you not live without? What makes your life easier? Do you even remember life before the PC?

Food: It brings us comfort; it brings us joy; it brings us together. Document both family recipes and food-sharing occasions.

Family Traditions: Create pages that include anything from weekend trips to the farmers market to celebrating the summer solstice.

Family Trees: Construct trees about your own lineage. (Future family genealogists will thank you!)

Family Heirlooms: Use items that have been passed down in your family as a vehicle to talk about family history. A dining room table, for example, can be the focus of a page detailing guests who have feasted there.

Homes, Neighborhoods and Towns: Do you ever wish you had a floor plan of Great Aunt Edna's stately Victorian or a detailed description of her town? Create pages that provide this information.

Occupations: Recount a typical day at the office or the trials and joys of being a stay-at-home mom.

A Day in the Life: Times are always changing, and scrapbook pages are terrific ways to keep a finger on the pulse of shifting lifestyles.

Hobbies: What you do in your spare time is a wonderful indicator of who you are. Detail how you discovered your passion, how much time you put into it and how it makes you feel.

Family Sayings: Did your father enjoy saying, "Let's hope it's a purple-elephant-in-a-tree day," (a magical, to-be-dreamed-about, one-of-a-kind special day)? Jot down the phrases unique to your family.

Be Creative

Scrapbooking provides a creative outlet that impacts emotional and spiritual well-being

when you were a baby, life was all about daddy. but for over two years now, you've been quite the mama's boy. i've just about given up on getting anything done around here. because if you are awake, you are my constant companion. and although i hate to say it, at 3 1/2, your help is not always very helpful. on this particular weekend, i had just sat down to read a magazine when i looked up to find this impish face perched upon my knees.

so if you grow up with childhood memories of a cluttered house, fingerprints on every available surface and crumbs on the floor, remember this face. because this is not the face of a little boy who wants to help mom clean house or leave her alone to read a magazine. this is the face of a boy who says, "i'm looking for some fun, and i'm not taking no for an answer!"

and who could resist a face like this anyway? certainly not me.

i love you connor. my little charmer.

august 2005

 charming

Susan Cyrus

Charming

Having been charmed out of downtime by this compelling little cherub, the artist found an outlet for her frustrations by creating this scrapbook page. The result is an open-hearted account that will continue to remind her to cherish these "oh-dear" moments.

Creativity involves breaking out of established patterns in order to look at things in a different way.

Edward De Bono

Many people don't think of themselves as creative until they find scrapbooking. It provides hesitant or intimidated creative spirits with the opportunity to make something beautiful. There are no "musts" in scrapbook art. It is successful because it is meaningful.

Art is the nonverbal communication of the subconscious mind, which makes it a useful tool in helping those struggling to identify their thoughts and feelings. The art of scrapbooking provides crafters with an opportunity to get in touch with their core. They are often surprised to find themselves reaching for papers in colors or styles they hadn't contemplated working with—papers that suddenly appear absolutely "right" for scrapbooking a particular photo once they allow themselves to listen to their subconscious.

The act of creating a scrapbook page offers mental refuge. Much like the act of creating a superb meal, you can gain focus on planning, shopping and preparation. For those hours and the ones that involve the creation of the piece, you take a holiday from the outside world and focus on the exciting task at hand.

Whether you are scrapbooking a landscape, a birthday party or your neighbor's child, your pages are really about you. The colors, the style, the topics you choose to scrapbook reflect your personality and how you perceive the world around you.

Heidi Schueller

Scrapbooks: A Timeless Tradition

Scrapbooks have been a trusty companion to cultures for many centuries, guarding memorabilia, showcasing inspirations and creativity and sharing personal reflections

Modern scrapbooking can be traced to the Renaissance, a time when people sought a means to collect inspirational quotes and literary passages. By the 17th century, these collections had evolved into "commonplace books," in which were recorded personal interests, thoughts and current events. A century later, William Granger published a book about the history of England with an appendix of extra illustrations. His later books included blank pages at the back ready to be personalized with a reader's own sketches and memorabilia.

During the 19th century, scrapbooking experienced a boom. It began with friendship books, in which friends shared designs made of woven hair accompanied by autographs and short poems. The term "scrapbook" grew from the colorful scraps of paper with which people decorated their books. Accounts of scrapbooking and how-to-scrapbook articles began to pop up in magazines as the fad spread.

SCRAPBOOKING THROUGH THE CENTURIES

14th – 18th centuries: People begin recording cultural and literary inspirations in small books, which become known as "commonplace books" in the 17th century. In the 18th century, William Granger publishes a history book with an appendix of blank pages, ready to be personalized.

19th century: Scrapbooking's popularity booms with diaries, journals and friendship albums. Albums feature embossed covers, engravings, illustrations and locks of hair.

1837: Modern photography is born when the ancient technology of the camera obscura synthesizes with developments involving photo-sensitive compounds. Louis Daguerre succeeds in creating images on silver-plated copper.

The first technique book appeared in 1826—John Poole wrote "Manuscript Gleanings and the Literary Scrapbook." Soon thereafter the first photo album hit the market along with products such as die cuts and stamps. The biggest spike in scrapbook evolution came in the late 1800s with the invention of the camera. Now, photos replaced illustrations and graphic representations.

The swelling interest in modern-day scrapbooking is credited to the Church of Jesus Christ of Latter Day Saints, which sponsors FamilySearch.org. This Web site is touted as "the largest collection of free family history, family tree and genealogy records in the world." The group's Web site, available to people of all denominations, states, "Every person is important," and that "Families are meant to be both sacred and eternal."

In the 1990s, the term "memory book" was coined and so was born today's form of scrapbooking. Creative Memories, a scrapbook product manufacturer, literally brought scrapbooking into the home with a party-based selling concept not much different from Tupperware. Niche magazines sprouted up, including *Memory Makers* and *Creating Keepsakes,* and both online and retail scrapbooking stores proved profitable. Scrapbook hobbyists began organizing crops, or social functions in which scrapbookers could get together to crop, or create pages. Internet communities started to flourish and soon scrapbooking became a worldwide crafting phenomenon.

1872: Mark Twain invents a series of scrapbooks for Brentano's Literary Emporium in New York City.

20th century: The Church of Jesus Christ of Latter Day Saints helps spawn modern-day scrapbooking by promoting genealogy research via FamilySearch.org.

Photograph of the Family History Library 8 by Intellectual Reserve, Inc.

Today: Scrapbooking is booming. Several scrapbooking magazines and companies are flourishing. The hobby has attracted enthusiasts at a feverish pace. Regular cropping sessions are a welcome escape from everyday life.

Scrapbooking: A Retrospective Look

Photos, journaling, paper and stickers were the elements found on earlier scrapbook pages—today, memories are preserved in increasingly imaginative ways

Heidi Schueller

1995

Early page design was simple. The focus of scrapbooking was to place photos within an archival environment intended to safeguard and preserve them.

1998

Scrapbookers began to experiment artistically, but page design remained simple, with the focus on preservation. The home-based-sales company Creative Memories became synonymous with creative scrapbooking.

Heidi Schueller

2000

The scrapbook community splits. While some scrapbook artists continue to dedicate themselves to the creation of relatively simple, archival-quality pages, others begin to explore different scrapbooking products and techniques. In the name of art, they turn to trendy materials that are not archival.

Heidi Schueller

Heidi Schueller

2005

Scrapbooking is at its most progressive. Not only is the craft a means to document history, it also provides a strong creative outlet. Pages include a variety of styles and techniques using materials purchased in hobby stores, hardware and fabric stores as well as antiques and household items.

The Many Faces of Fashionable Pages

Scrapbooking is a progressive hobby, and today's scrapbook style cannot be defined by a single pattern or look

Wendy Chang

Shabby Chic

Shabby-chic style involves distressing techniques, found objects, mixing patterns and textures with feminine sensibilities and floral motifs. The colors are soft and subdued. It tends to incorporate fabric and sewing techniques.

Shabby-chic style allows the seamless mixing of a lifetime of craft obsessions and flea-market collecting. The textures and colors perfectly complement just about any photo.

Wendy Chang

Altered

Altered artists love distressed looks, but where shabby chic favors white-washing, altered favors coffee or tea staining. Altered art relies on recycled items, most commonly books and magazine clippings. Colors are rich and warm, and text patterns rule. Image transfers are a popular technique.

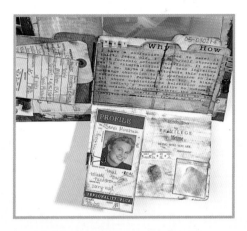

Sandy Minchuk

Niki Meiners

Grunge

Grunge scrapbooking is the happy union of shabby-chic and altered art. It is anything soft and feminine (shabby chic) that is not afraid to get dirty (altered). Hallmarks of the style include inked anything, contrasting textures (silk fabric with hard metal accents) and mixing funky font styles, colors and patterns.

Catherine Esta

Graphic

Graphic pages are clean and straightforward, taking their cue from print media. Magazines are true treasure troves for creative inspiration with their offerings of graphically designed advertisements. Most of the page designs feature photos and text logically organized into blocks.

Elegant

Elegant pages rely on classic patterns and motifs to create timeless effects. Toile patterns, ornate florals and graceful stripes keep elegant pages in high style.

Kate Childers

Eclectic

If a scrapbook page contains equal parts flea-market finds, craft-store supplies and hardware, its style is eclectic. This style is popular with those who cannot be confined to a particular style. It hinges on a successful mixture of unexpected elements.

Julie Johnson

Computer-Generated

Computer-generated pages usher in a new-age style where anything is possible. The artist has complete creative control and can manipulate images for artistic effect. Page accents can mimic lifelike counterparts such as brads, or be completely contrived.

Michelle Shefveland

Create Lasting Images

Great scrapbook pages begin with great photos

The shutter clicks, and a moment is captured. The photograph recalls an indelible memory for the photographer and allows her to share that memory. When this photo is joined by others in an album, they tell a story of the life of the scrapbooker and those who have shared it.

Photography is an interactive art form. The photographer orchestrates a dance in which subject and light are interwoven. As they progress through natural shifts, the mood of their interaction changes. It is the photographer's job to determine the moment in which the two synchronize most beautifully. It is that moment that calls to be commemorated in a photo.

As in most art forms, good photographers must know how to select their tools—cameras, lighting equipment, film—and how those tools work. They must learn to interact with their subjects, select locations and work through unexpected challenges. Learning to become a better photographer is the first step to learning to be a strong scrapbooker. On the following pages, you'll find the information you need to become both.

So delve into this chapter and delve into the exciting world of photography, where with the press of a button you can freeze special times—your child's smile or embrace—on photos that will warm your heart.

Lisa VanderVeen

A good snapshot stops a moment from running away.

Eudora Welty

Get to Know Your Camera

Unlock your camera's potential by spending some time with it and the owner's manual

Few things are more exciting, useful and valuable to a scrapbooker than her camera. It is her personal memory catcher. But, these little black boxes of electronics can mystify even the most intrepid souls. The first step to taking stronger photos is getting better acquainted with your camera. Grab your camera and the owner's manual and dedicate a Sunday morning to reading up on its features. Your grade-A photos will be testimony to your time spent studying.

Camera Choices

When purchasing a camera, consider your needs. Do you want a sophisticated camera capable of professional-quality images, something simple or a camera that fits in between those two? The versatile photographer will want to own more than one camera—a small compact and a more versatile camera such as an SLR with interchangeable lenses. Keep a single-use camera on hand to use when harsh conditions, such as the sand and water of a beach, could damage an expensive camera.

POINT-AND-SHOOT VS. AN SLR

One is fully automatic; one gives you total control. Both have pros and cons.

Point-and-shoot

- Easy to use: literally point and shoot

- Lightweight, small and portable

- Inexpensive

- No control over exposure

- Resulting photograph not always what is seen through viewfinder

- Unable to enhance with interchangeable lenses

SLR (single lens reflex)

- Multiple-exposure modes make for maximum creative control

- Interchangeable lenses

- Image viewed through actual lens for precise framing

- Larger and heavier

- More challenging to master

Camera Control Basics

Like all technology, cameras have come a long way. This is a brief list of features that the new camera buyer should include on their "must have" list of camera controls. If you already own a camera, check the owner's manual to learn about the controls your camera has to offer.

Auto focus This function allows you to shoot continuously without stopping to focus your camera.

Long exposure or nighttime mode When trying to photograph bright lights against a night sky (for example, a fireworks display), this function is invaluable.

Automatic exposure modes These exposure modes range from the simple "program" mode to specific subject modes (for example, "landscape") designed for different exposure situations. You'll learn more about exposure modes later in this chapter.

Self-timer or infrared remote shutter release Should the photographer wish to be included in the picture, a self timer gives the photographer a short delay before the camera takes the photo. An infrared remote allows the photographer to stand away from the camera and take a photo by just pressing a button on the remote.

Fill flash If your camera has a built-in flash, this feature allows the photographer to artfully mix available light with flash.

Celeste Smith

Sam

Proper understanding of your camera and its functions will result in better photographs. For this portrait, the artist set her camera to portrait mode to ensure the adorable subject would be shot in sharp focus.

Lenses

The lens is largely responsible for the sharpness and contrast of a photograph. Light, the main ingredient in a photo, enters the lens, which, along with the shutter, controls the amount of light that reaches the film or digital sensor. The lens also impacts how large the subject can be reproduced. SLR cameras have interchangeable lenses, which gives the photographer access to a wide range of focal lengths. Point-and-shoot cameras usually have a fixed focal length lens or a zoom, limiting their flexibility. No matter what type of camera you use, take care when handling lenses; their glass "eyes" are very sensitive to scratches. Never clean a lens with your finger, and only use products approved by the manufacturer for cleaning.

Photos: Andrea Zocchi

Focal Lengths

The wide-angle shot (far left) captures more visual information and creates a sense of distance between the photographer and the buildings. The normal lens (middle) replicates the image seen by the naked eye. When shot with a telephoto lens (far right), the buildings appear tighter and closer to the photographer.

Five Basic Lens Types

Each of these basic lens types creates a unique photo effect.

Normal An all-purpose normal lens (50mm to 55mm) sees what the human eye sees.

Wide-angle When you need to capture larger images such as architecture or vast landscapes, wide-angle lenses are a good choice. They come in a variety of sizes, but 24mm, 28mm, and 35mm are the most common.

Zoom Zoom lenses allow the photographer to change the focal length of the lens. There are zooms that cover a range from wide angle to medium telephoto. A zoom is a great choice if you only want to carry one lens to take a variety of photos.

Telephoto This lens magnifies the image, making the object you are photographing appear closer than it really is. It also creates a narrower view and compresses space.

Macro When you want to shoot in sharp focus at very close range, opt for a macro lens. This lens allows you to fill the image frame with something small, such as an insect.

THE SPEED OF FILM

Choose the correct speed of film for different photo situations (Digital camera owners: Don't forget, you probably have an ISO setting on your camera to allow you to do this). You'll need to consider the amount of light and the activity level of the photo subjects. (Will they be stationary or moving?)

Slow (100 - 200 ISO) If there will be a lot of light, opt for slower film.

Medium (400 ISO) This is all-purpose film. If you are ever in doubt, choose it. It works well outdoors if the light is not too bright nor too dark.

Fast (800 ISO and higher) For low-light situations or those with fast-moving subjects, you'll need faster film.

All the Pretty Horses

To capture the full breadth and beauty of this carrousel, the artist took photos from different angles and ranges. The result is a scrapbook page that tells the story from varied perspectives and shows many details of the horses.

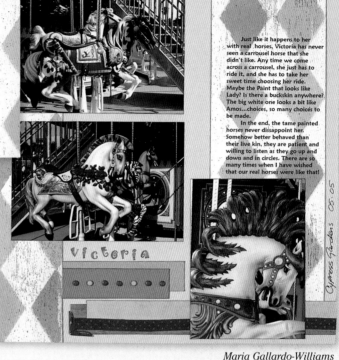

Just like it happens to her with real horses, Victoria has never seen a carrousel horse that she didn't like. Any time we come across a carrousel, she just has to ride it, and she has to take her sweet time choosing her ride. Maybe the Paint that looks like Lady? Is there a buckskin anywhere? The big white one looks a bit like Amos...choices, so many choices to be made.

In the end, the tame painted horses never disappoint her. Somehow better behaved than their live kin, they are patient and willing to listen as they go up and down and in circles. There are so many times when I have wished that our real horses were like that!

Maria Gallardo-Williams

A PHOTOGRAPHER'S ACCESSORIES

A camera is just the starting point when it comes to "must-have" tools for a photographer. Here are a few other investments that will protect your prized equipment, keep you organized and help you create better photos.

Camera bag Protect your camera with a camera bag that is sufficiently padded and has adjustable straps. (Padded straps will make carrying heavy equipment more comfortable.) Look for bags with enough compartments to keep you organized. Before you buy a bag, lay out all of your camera equipment and supplies to determine the size you will need. Then compare brands and prices before purchasing.

Camera strap You know what they say, "An ounce of prevention is worth a pound of cure." Buy a good quality, comfortable camera strap and use it 100 percent of the time.

Tripod Serious photographers must own a tripod. It holds your camera still, which makes it a necessity for shooting with a slow shutter speed. A cable release is also a good addition. It attaches to your camera for remote shutter release, reducing vibration.

UV filters UV filters can be purchased at most camera stores. Buy one for every lens you own. Filters protect your lenses from dust and scratches, can be used to manipulate images, help optimize color, eliminate glare and increase detail. Also many a photographer has dropped or banged her camera lens to find that the UV filter broke but the lens was unhurt.

Understand Exposure

Know the basics and take control of your camera

Henri Cartier-Bresson, one of the world's greatest photographers, called that split second when everything comes together in a photograph "the decisive moment." To make sure you are ready to capture your "decisive moment," you need to know the basics of exposure. Exposure is the amount of light used to create a photograph. Photos that are properly exposed received the requisite amount of light needed. Overexposed and underexposed images received either too much or too little light. Several camera controls affect exposure. The information on the next four pages will teach you how to best use those controls.

Aperture

To properly expose a photograph, you must first understand aperture and shutter speed. Aperture controls light, and light is the magic that creates a photograph. Imagine that the lens is the eye of the camera and the aperture is the pupil, controlling the amount of light that enters the camera. A diaphragm within the camera lens determines the aperture. It can be made larger or smaller to let in more or less light.

Proper aperture selection results in images with a full tonal range. This means that detail is present in every area of the photograph, no matter how bright the highlights or how dark the shadows. A properly exposed image has no large, solid black areas devoid of detail and no large, solid, "super nova" bright white areas.

Aperture is measured in f-stops. Here's where it gets tricky. SMALLER apertures have bigger numbers. In other words, an aperture of F22 is a smaller aperture than F4. Likewise, an aperture of F22 allows less light to enter the camera lens than F4. In other words, when you are photographing in very bright conditions you need a small aperture like F16 and in low-light conditions you need a large aperture like F4.5.

Depth of Field

Aperture also determines depth of field, or what portions of your image will be in focus. Small apertures, F22 or F16, result in a wide depth of field, making both close and far objects in focus, as seen in the photo below. If, for example, you are creating a landscape image with trees in the foreground and a snow-capped mountain in the distance, you want a small aperture. Large apertures, F2.8 or F4.0, result in a very shallow depth of field, meaning that a shallow plane of the photograph will be in focus. Shallow depth of field is ideal when making a portrait. If you focus on your subject's eyes, the background will soften and blur, and your subject will be in focus.

Photo: Andrea Zocchi

Three

This stunning image of a toddler's face was created by using a shallow depth of field. A shallow depth of field results in a sharply focused foreground image in front of a softly blurred background.

It's hard to believe that on this day next month you'll be three. You'll grow even more independent, go to school, use the potty — become a big boy. It's hard to see, to realize, and to accept. But I'll get used to being the mommy of a three year old...in about a mo

Marla Kress

Shutter Speed

The second camera mechanism that controls exposure is the shutter. The shutter is like a curtain that can open for a longer time (a slow shutter speed), or a shorter time (a fast shutter speed). Shutter speeds are measured in seconds and fractions of a second. The "average" shutter speed is 1/125 of a second. This speed compensates for any subtle movement that would otherwise result in a blurry photo.

Using a slow shutter speed—from about 1/60 of a second to several minutes—requires a tripod to prevent even the tiniest camera movement that will result in blurry images.

A fast shutter speed of 1/250 of a second to 1/1000 of a second or higher is great for shooting moving subjects, such as a child at play. The shutter speed freezes motion, in addition to controlling how much light to which the film or digital sensor is exposed. If this seems confusing, try this experiment: Pretend your eyelids are a shutter. Without blinking, move your head quickly from side to side. Notice how it is hard to focus and how things look blurry? Now move your head again, while blinking rapidly. See how your vision registers separate, in-focus images? That's how a shutter works!

Photo: Andrea Zocchi

How to Use Exposure Controls

Now that you understand the terms "aperture," "depth of field" and "shutter speed," the function of those camera exposure controls will become clear.

Manual Control

To achieve a good photo in manual mode, mentally compose your shot, paying particular attention to the range of colors within the image. Identify the mid tones (those that are not too bright nor too dark). Fill the camera's viewfinder with the area of the image containing the mid tones. Adjust the aperture and shutter speed until the camera meter signals a proper exposure. Recompose your photo and shoot.

Aperture Priority

Using this semiautomatic mode, the photographer sets the desired aperture (f-stop), and the camera automatically chooses the correct shutter speed. This mode is best used in medium to bright light in which there is little danger of blur or camera shake due to a slow shutter speed. This mode is terrific when you wish to control your depth of field.

Shutter Priority

Shutter priority is also a semiautomatic mode. Simply set the shutter speed and the camera automatically selects the aperture. Shutter priority is great for freezing action such as sporting events. Be sure to focus accurately when operating your camera in shutter priority. Dim light conditions result in a shallow depth of field.

Program Mode

Program is the fully automatic, point-and-shoot mode. Today's best cameras have very sophisticated program modes that actually measure the light in a number of areas within your scene, resulting in good photos most of the time. The only negative to program mode is that it attempts to create an image with a "full tonal range" for all shots—even when you might prefer otherwise. For example, you might wish to silhouette your subject against a brilliant sunset. However, if using program mode, your sunset will look washed out while your subject appears a little dark. In this situation only manual mode will deliver the desired results.

If manual mode and the semiautomatic modes are still intimidating, set your camera on program and use the exposure compensation feature. (Check your owner's manual to see if your camera has this feature.) Exposure compensation allows you to increase or decrease exposure in small increments, supplying a measure of creative control without leaving the fully automatic comfort of program mode.

Subject Modes

Subject modes are those little icons on the exposure mode dial/control. In their little "international symbol" way, they automatically control the exposure to favor particular shots. For example, the photograph below was taken in the "landscape" mode with a compact digital camera. The landscape mode is best for images that require the foreground, middle ground and background each to be in sharp focus. Depending upon your camera, these subject modes may be very sophisticated or simple. In high-end SLRs, they can change the auto-focus pattern and the film advance speed. If you are a program-mode-only photographer, subject modes will help you achieve better results.

Photo: Andrea Zocchi

Put Me in Coach

The feeling of capturing a great action shot at a sporting event is just as exhilarating as the game itself because it is such a challenge. Superb action shots need speed—fast film, fast shutter speed, fast trigger finger—and good light. Add a little luck, be in the right place at the right time, and you've got your shot.

Syalynne Kramer

Recognize Light Quality

Learn to manipulate the most important factor in photography

The term "photography" has Greek origins. Literally translated, it means "to write with light." Every time you press the shutter release on your camera, you are using light to create an image. Your photos will improve as you become more aware of the light around you and how it affects objects it touches. Begin by putting aside worries about the amount of light available and focus on the quality of that light. When possible, take advantage of natural light rather than relying on ambient or artificial light, such as your camera's flash. Natural light complements skin tones, making your photo subjects look their best.

Two Different Types of Light

Light, while a generic term, comes in a rainbow of varieties. It can be tinted or reflected to produce warmer or brighter rays. But when evaluating light for your photographs, learn to distinguish between hard and soft light.

Hard light comes from a direct source, meaning it is not reflected or diffused. Your camera's flash, the light from an unshaded light bulb and the sun all produce hard light. Hard light creates a definite contrast between light and shadow. It works best to convey strong feelings or energy. If used incorrectly, hard light will steal the definition and detail from your image and create unforgiving shadows.

Soft light is indirect, having been "softened" through reflection or diffusion. Sunlight filtered by the shade of trees or clouds on an overcast day is soft. So is hard light reflected against a wall from a window. Soft light evens the contrast between light and shadow and is very flattering for photographing people.

How can I turn hard light into soft light?

Reflect the light with a solid piece of foam core or a white sheet. Or, if outdoors during a sunny day, position photo subjects beneath the shade of a tree. Seek indirect light from a window (see the photo to the right), or photograph in a garage with the door open. In fact, garages make excellent home studios. Simply clear a corner, hang a sheet as a backdrop, pose your subject and begin shooting.

Photo: Andrea Zocchi

The Color of Light

Have you ever noticed how a beautiful sunset touches everything with a golden glow? The light of a sunset is markedly different from the light emitted by the harsh sunlight at high noon. In the same manner, indoor light varies from location to location. Office spaces tend to be illuminated by sterile light emitted from a fluorescent bulb while homes are more often warmed by the cozy light of an incandescent bulb.

As a photographer, take note of the color of the light around you. Notice if you are working with cool light versus warm. If you are hoping to capture warm and gilded skins tones, stay away from artificial light and strong sunlight. Instead, opt for natural light at dawn or dusk. Choosing the correct temperature of light for your photos will give them a natural ambience and complement the desired mood.

Light Changes Quickly

These two photographs were taken less than 20 minutes apart on a chilly Christmas day. Notice the warm light in the photo on the left. However as soon as the low winter sun sank behind a cloud, the light turned a cold blue color.

Photos: Andrea Zocchi

Photo: Andrea Zocchi

Capture the Color of Light

A gold mask in a store window in Venice looks even more golden when illuminated by incandescent light. The shop window spotlights create a yellow/gold color. Our eyes adjust for this coloration, but daylight film sees it as it actually is.

The Direction of Light

Did you ever sit in a darkened room while a storyteller spun a ghost tale? Scary! Even scarier when the storyteller holds a flashlight to his chin, shining it so that a strong beam of light bathes his cheekbones and forehead, leaving the eyes dark in the recesses of a shadow. While this shivery lighting effect is perfect for things-that-go-bump-in-the-night moments, it would not be a good choice for a portrait!

Just as the direction of light affects the mood of a moment, it affects the mood of a photograph. Below are lighting techniques that rely on direction to create a desired effect.

Silhouette A solid black shape against a detailed background is a dramatic image. To create it, you need bright light. The light source must come from behind the subject.

Top Lighting When a subject is bathed in light from above, harsh shadows can form. Try angling the light toward the subject at 45- or 90-degree angles for Rembrandt lighting. (Perfect for celebrating wisdom-wrinkles in an older subject or highlighting missing teeth in children.)

Side Lighting When light comes from the side, shadows and highlights are enhanced. Correct side lighting results in detailed images that appear dimensional.

Back Lighting To create a glowing golden backdrop, the main source of light must come from behind the subject (as in the bicycle photo below). To capture detail on the front of the subject, the foreground must also be sufficiently lit.

Flat Lighting This light hits the subject dead on. Use diffused light for best results.

Photo: Andrea Zocchi

Photo: Joann Zocchi

+Q&a

What causes glasses-glare and how can I avoid it?

The reflection of the flash on the lenses of the glasses causes the glare. The easiest way to avoid it is to turn off the flash. That means you need to have plenty of light to create the photo. If you must use the flash, reduce reflection by asking the subject to angle her head downward.

Electronic Flash

Many photography enthusiasts will denounce the use of a flash as "too bright, too artificial, too unflattering." But, proper understanding and use of the flash can result in serendipitous usage. Using a flash can also allow you to create an image under otherwise impossible lighting conditions. For example, small babies rarely wait for proper lighting conditions to do something extraordinarily cute, so thank God for camera flash. This crotchety crawler, on the page shown right, was caught squirming on the kitchen floor, his telling expressions caught by the grace of the flash.

Jennifer Gallacher

Red-Eye Reduction

While some family members may tease that red-eyed relatives are simply...well...less than angelic, the real cause of demonic eyes is the reflection of a flash bouncing off of retinas. Try to avoid the need for a flash by increasing the amount of ambient light in the room. Asking photo subjects to divert their eyes away from the lens of the camera may also help. If your flash is connected to your camera via a synch cord rather than directly attached, try bouncing the flash off of the ceiling or another reflective surface. Red-eye-reduction modes are also a handy tool.

Photo: Andrea Zocchi

Mix Natural and Artificial Light

Flash can balance natural light by filling in shadows. In fact, the fill-flash setting on your camera was designed as natural light's little helper, emitting just enough light to augment natural (and ambient) light. The photo on the left utilized fill-flash to illuminate the subject and prevent him from disappearing into the dark shadows of late afternoon.

Natural and artificial light also can be combined for artistic effect. Artificial light, your flash included, has a tendency to be cooler in color temperature. Try combining the brake lights of zooming cars with the light from a cresting dawn.

Compose Simply Beautiful Images
These tools will take you from snapping pictures to making great photographs

The most stunning images are often the most simple. They engage the eye with a strong focal point, an uncluttered foreground and a background rich with color and texture. When composing a photograph, your goal is to construct an image that grabs the eye and guides it toward points of interest. When framing an image, make sure that everything you see when peering through the viewfinder adds to, rather than distracts from, the shot.

Think of a photograph as having three parts: the foreground, the middle ground and the background. The focal point of the image most often resides in the middle ground and should be supported rather than overpowered by the foreground and background. Use the foreground to draw a viewer into the scene, establish scale or guide the eye with the presence of a strong shape, line, color or texture. The background is the scenery. Use it to create a backdrop full of detail and context, provide depth or help define the subject.

Photo: Andrea Zocchi

Use the Rule of Thirds

In composition, the "rule of thirds" mandates that images balance each other on an imaginary grid. When composing an image, pretend a grid consisting of nine equal rectangles set in three rows and three columns (in Tic-Tac-Toe fashion) rests over your camera's viewfinder. Center the focal point of your image on any of the intersecting lines. This will create dynamic tension between the subject and the rest of the image.

Photo: Andrea Zocchi

Frame the Shot

Subject matter determines the most complementary camera angle to use when taking a photo. Vertical camera angles are perfect for slender, narrow subjects such as tall buildings or a single long-stem rose as well as anything in which you want to portray height. Landscapes, groups of people and times when you wish to portray width are best complemented by horizontal camera angles. When composing an image, experiment with both angles to achieve best results.

Allow Color to Influence Mood

Carefully considering color when composing a photo can result in an image that exudes appropriate emotion. Because each color emotionally impacts us differently— hot colors such as red make our hearts race while cool blues and greens calm—select hues that support your creative intention.

When you are scouting a scene for a photo, look at the colors around you. Will the weathered red of a wooden door under a smoky stone buttress help convey the visual story of Argentine architecture? Will the earth tones of Mother Nature breathe lush life into your memories of Yellowstone? Will the harmonious blend of golden haystacks and orange pumpkins whisk you back to a fall festival? You bet!

Photo: Joann Zocchi

Linda Sobolewski

Totally Girl

The calming blue of lapping waves imparts an unquestionable sense of serenity on this page. The artist took advantage of a quiet and unpopulated beach as a backdrop for this contemplative portrait.

Find Patterns, Shapes and Textures

Conceptualization of art often begins with a basic shape or the quality of a line, whether smooth and contoured or jagged and rough. Simple shapes, interesting lines, repeating patterns and provocative textures add visual value to an image, just as they add interest to works of art and well-designed graphics. Learn to identify and appreciate these features by focusing on the details of objects around you, such as the circular form of radiating flower petals, the sharp edges of cliffs or a row of antique cars set in a syncopated pattern.

Photos: Joann Zocchi

Re-awaken the Senses

Water is a subject worthy of a million photographs. Here, the artist uses a series of textural waterfall images on a rustic page.

Anita Mundt

When composing a scenic shot, where should the horizon line fall?

If you want to draw attention to the middle and foreground of the scene, using the rule of thirds, position the horizon in the top one-third of the image. If you want to focus on the sky, run the horizon along the bottom one-third of the image. Avoid placing the horizon line in the middle of the image. It will result in an uninspiring photograph.

Get Close

Close-up images are simple yet enchanting, filling the frame and eliminating distracting backgrounds. Close-up images command attention and hold a viewer's gaze. You can achieve a close-up photograph by physically moving closer to your subject or moving your subject closer to you. You may also use a zoom lens or macro setting on your camera. Tightly cropping an image also achieves a close-up effect.

Angie Head

Snow

This image resulted from the combined use of a zoom lens, a photographer in close proximity to the subject and an effective crop. A zoom lens allows you to visually move in on your subject. Zoom lenses are sold with a wide range of focal lengths.

Friendship

The main image on this scrapbook page is so compelling it halts the viewer in her tracks. The photo was taken outside on an overcast day. The soft light created smooth, even skin tones. Keep in mind that lighting is very important when taking close-up shots because a magnified image results in dramatic contrast between light and shadow.

Jamie Tharpe

READY TO SHOOT A CLOSE-UP?

Simple tips for great close-up photographs

- Soft light is the most flattering. Look for a north-facing window or a diffused light source.

- Longer focal-length lenses improve portraits. Stay away from wide-angle lenses as they make faces look round and noses clownlike.

- Use a tripod if possible, to prevent a blurry image.

- Be aware of any shadows you might create as the photographer.

Change Your Perspective

Quick, grab a pencil and paper. It's time for a pop quiz! Question: What's one of the easiest ways to increase intensity, emotion and energy in your photographs?

If you answered "by changing the perspective," you are correct! Perspective, also known as "point of view," is the angle from which a picture is taken. Changing perspective can dramatically alter your final product.

Photo: Andrea Zocchi

Photo: Andrea Zocchi

Look Up, Look Down

Why do all those tourists climb to the top of the bell tower? The answer is "point of view." So when you are at the top, stop and take a photo and don't forget to look down.

Linda Sobolewski

Sisters, Friends

Captivating images needn't always include adorable faces. Arms connecting two bodies, two heads tilted inward, two pair of feet walking in step, two backs wrapped in the same swimsuit speak to the closeness of the subjects. Those details, as seen in this photograph, make it clear that these subjects share a very special bond.

Manipulate Scale

Scale, or the relationship between the sizes of two photographic subjects, can show depth, underscore the actual size of an object or create an illusion. You might creatively utilize the concept of scale, for example, in a photo that shows a model trying to wrap her arms around the massive girth of a towering redwood tree. Such a photo would establish the true size of the trunk. Use scale in your photography for dramatic results.

Daughter of Mine

The size of the tiny infant's foot is emphasized when cradled in the mother's hand.

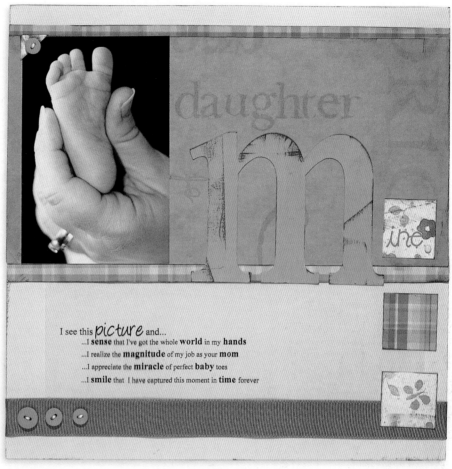

I see this *picture* and...
...I **sense** that I've got the whole **world** in my **hands**
...I realize the **magnitude** of my job as your **mom**
...I appreciate the **miracle** of perfect **baby** toes
...I **smile** that I have captured this moment in **time** forever

Tracy Kuethe

Photo: Joann Zocchi

A VARIETY OF SCALE

Two types of scale can be used to create dynamic images.

Spacial scale Use spacial scale to create depth within a image. To create deep space, compose an image so that the images in the foreground are larger than those in the background.

Comparative scale To enhance the actual size of an object, relate it to an object that is either bigger or smaller than it.

Tell a Story with a Photo Series

Photo essays tell a visual story through a series of images. Like most well-constructed stories, the photo essay has a beginning, middle and end. The series of photos also includes a climactic focal photo, supported by a cast of detail shots. Detail shots may include close-ups and environment scenes that provide context for the story.

When creating a photo essay, make sure you have photos of all the characters involved, including the "heroes" and the opposition. You should have "before" and "after" pictures of the event as well as photos of the story unfolding. Your finished set of photos should include posed images as well as action and candid shots.

A series of photos taken over time also can be used to create a photo essay. For example, a series of school portraits may be featured on a scrapbook page celebrating a child's high-school career. Similar pages utilizing photos that show growth and accomplishment might also be created for anniversaries and retirements.

Samuel Cole

Base, Safe, Run, Catch

This collection of photos shows a triumphant child succeeding at team sports. The artist was sure to capture all of the action moments.

PHOTO ESSAYS: THE THEME OF THINGS

Here's a list of page ideas perfect for creating photo essays. Don't forget to photograph the preparation for these events.

- Sporting events
- A day in the life
- Anniversaries
- Retirements
- Pregnancies
- Weddings
- Holidays
- First day of school

- Home remodeling projects
- Neighbor/block parties
- Vacations
- First experiences (especially for babies)
- Family reunions
- Tribute pages
- Adventures (hiking, skiing, rafting, etc.)
- Community events such as charity fundraisers

Look for Details

Without detail photos, scrapbook pages can be flat, lifeless and dull. Detail shots demand that viewers take a hard look at things you consider important. Your detail shots can be close-up images or capture a wider view of a piece of scenery that was overshadowed by the focal point within a larger shot.

Jane Davies

Ephesus

Sometimes beautiful vistas and dramatic landscapes are too big to capture in one frame. Here, the artist created a detailed photo essay of these ancient Turkish ruins by focusing on the elements of the crumbling architecture. By doing so, the reader is able to enjoy chiseled images and textures.

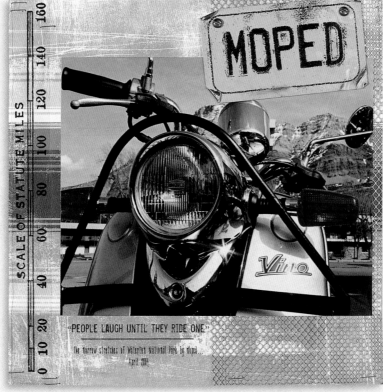

Mary MacAskill

Moped

The chrome and steel of this moped make for a terrific focal-point photo on this page. The photographer makes the moped look more sophisticated and imposing by moving in close for a detail shot.

Focus on Your Loved Ones

How to turn a snapshot into an indelible image

Photographing people is one of the most rewarding and challenging endeavors under-taken by any photographer. People can be "on" or "off" depending upon the moment. They tend to interact with the photographer, looking for direction and support. A good photographer has the technical know-how and savvy that can set a subject at ease, unleashing her personality and capturing her—heart and soul.

Shannon Taylor

Almost Grown

These photos are a testament to this young model's blossoming womanhood. The artist and photographer staged an impromptu photo shoot with the girl after a dance recital, while still fresh in her makeup. The model's Egyptian eyes made the artist sigh at the fact that the girl is on her way to becoming a woman.

Happy Kidz

Encourage your subject's true self to shine when taking photos. If the subject wants to be silly, indulge him. If the subject is more somber, refrain from demanding smiles.

Samuel Cole

BRINGING OUT THE BEST IN PEOPLE

Expert tips for creating people-shots with personality

Focus on the eyes They are the windows to the soul.

Encourage interaction Allow groups of people to interact to avoid static portraiture.

Prevent height distortion When photographing a standing subject, hold the camera parallel to the subject's waist to prevent a distorted image.

Turn your camera Try both vertical and horizontal shots. Angle the camera to add zing to a shot.

Get closer Physically move closer to your subject. Zoom in on small details.

Get photos from all angles Don't limit photos to straight-on face shots. Try profile shots or ask the subject to turn around to capture broad, strong shoulders.

Be sneaky Take candid photos of an unsuspecting family member. Casually snap photos with the camera at chest level while you engage the subject in conversation.

Move Don't be stationary. Move while snapping away. If in a studio environment, use a stepladder or chair to get shots from higher angles. Belly up to the floor for a new perspective.

Engage the subject Make your subjects laugh with silly stories. Ask them questions for thoughtful poses. Have them do long division for a face full of intensity.

Be open to ideas Listen to your subject's idea for a pose or perspective.

Use props Your subject may be more comfortable when holding a book or treasured trophy. This is especially important for babies and small children.

Have snacks Hungry photo subjects are cranky photo subjects. Have clean refreshments available.

Be prepared Be ready to snap away when your subject arrives. Have extra film and batteries on hand.

Schedule enough time Let your subject know you'll need about an hour to complete the photo shoot.

Photo: Joann Zocchi

Highlight a Personality

Successfully photographing a person requires a level of trust between the photographer and subject. Encouraging a subject to shine is a process that unfolds, requiring patience on the part of the photographer and trust on the part of the model.

Being prepared for your photo session is a key to making it successful. Before your model arrives, consider the image you hope to capture and create a list of words that best describe your concept. How can you help your subject exhibit those qualities during the shoot?

Begin the shoot by breaking the ice between you and your subject by chatting for a few minutes. Keep the conversation going as you photograph. Pull the camera away from your face from time to time to speak to the subject. As you are snapping, vary the subject's poses as well as your camera controls.

Laura McKinley

Happiness Is...

This photo captures this small boy's pure delight. Whether you are conducting a formal photo shoot or simply lucky enough to catch a memorable candid, the best photos will result when your subject feels comfortable and natural.

How can I encourage a child to be more cooperative during a photo shoot?

Cooperation is dependent on the mood of your young photo subject. Gain your subject's trust and make him feel comfortable. Kneel down and talk to him on his level. Be silly, play games and give him toys to play with. Have lots of film handy to compensate for fidgets and blinks. Be prepared to snap at any moment. Avoid wardrobe changes as they can be a surefire way to introduce the crankies.

I Am Amazed by You

This close-up image shows a confident, content and strong young boy. Outside, seated in the grass and wearing his favorite cap, his pose is natural and his face relaxed. When shooting a subject, be mindful of familiar locations that will set him at ease.

Amber Clark

She Is Our Princess

Moments of glee and high energy are fleeting. This artist was ready with her camera to capture a cheery young model reacting to a joyful occasion.

Linda Sobolewski

GO ON A GENDER BENDER

Use these tricks to bring out the best in male and female subjects.

Females

- Tilt chin down for a more demure appearance.
- Use a higher camera angle to enhance a delicate frame.
- Angle the shoulders slightly toward the camera for a slimming effect.

Males

- Square their shoulders toward the camera to enhance a powerful build.
- Shoot male subjects at an upward angle.
- Allow men to lean on something, such as a fence or against a wall. It will help them to relax and give you their best.

Define Relationships

Too often, group photos look more like group mug shots than informal portraits. Create more compelling group photos by setting your subjects in a comfortable environment with a simple background. Engage them while photographing, and encourage them to interact both physically and emotionally with each other. Look for nuances in body language, such as gentle squeezes, longing looks or comforting hand pats, and capture the moment in your image.

Shelly Boyd

Jonathan and Tubby

This snuggly portrait shows the thoughtful and caring relationship between a boy and his new puppy. To capture the moment, the artist got down on the floor to shoot the two-some at eye level. The result is a warm image that tugs at your heart.

Arrange Stunning Group Shots

Group shots are ubiquitous mementos of most social gatherings including weddings, graduations, holidays and family reunions. Too often, the call for a group shot is met with groans and the resulting images look like an unhappy group of cattle herded together for branding. The victims have closed eyes, their mouths are open in comment and hind quarters are turned toward the camera.

Reduce complaints about group photos by informing participants about what you plan to do, how you plan to achieve your goal and how long it will take. Next, arrange the group. Think simple shapes, such as a circle (mid-height people flank taller people and shorter people are in front) or triangle (taller people in the back, shorter in the front). Make sure everyone can see you and your camera. If the group is large and you have a wide-angle lens, use it. It will help you get closer to the group.

Photo: Joann Zocchi

Now, make things fun. After you've snapped the traditional "smile for the camera" shots, start telling jokes while you casually take photos. Ask everyone to jump up and down and get some action shots. Don't forget to use your tripod and self-timer so you can participate in the shot as well!

Capture Candids

Capturing great candid photos is as much an endeavor guided by luck and stealth as it is an art. Photographers who consistently snap strong candid pictures are almost always sneaky. They distance themselves from subjects and start snapping before their presence is discovered. A wide-angle lens allows the photographer to fool shy subjects by pointing the camera away while keeping them in the far end of the frame. In the page to the right, the photographer wasn't so much stealthy as she was simply ready to catch her toddler in an endearing moment.

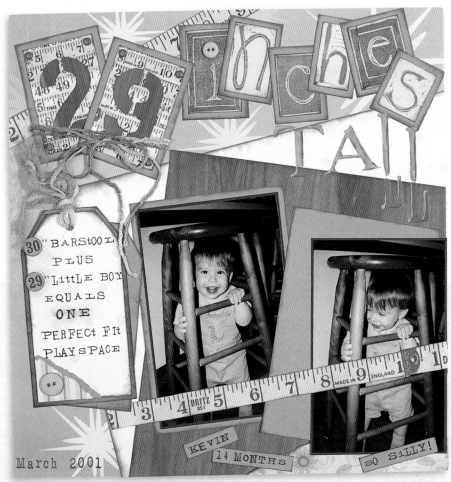

Madeline Fox

Photo: Joann Zocchi

LOCATION, LOCATION, LOCATION

How to scout a choice environment for your subjects.

Keep it comfortable Make sure the environment isn't too hot, too bright, too dark nor too humid.

Pick a familiar setting A favorite park or Grandma's porch will put your subject at ease. Be sure to position your subject in front of a simple background.

Pick the perfect time of day Keep the light in mind when choosing a setting. If outdoors, opt for morning or late afternoon light, or find a shady spot to filter bright sunlight. Avoid high-stress times of day, such as just before dinner. This will ensure a more relaxed subject.

Mark Your Memories with Words

Delight in telling the tales of your memories

It could be said that journaling saves lives...or at least the details and stories of those who have lived. Those details and stories are the color and shading that fill in the sketchy outlines of our ancestors. Journaling brings them to life, providing rich texture—a heartbeat to which we can relate.

Photos capture images of people, places, things and events. Good photos do more than simply record these subjects. They evoke emotion. What they may not do is expose what is invisible to the lens' eye—the thoughts and feelings of the photographer and photo subjects. They may also fail to provide details such as the names of those in the photos, circumstances and dates. The written word is necessary to recount all this information. When words join photos on a scrapbook page, wonderful things happen.

A well-journaled scrapbook page can close the gap of generations and allow others to meet our ancestors. A well-journaled page can allow future generations to know us. And because words laid down upon paper are more resilient than our memories, they help us retain details of events we long to hold close to our hearts throughout our own lifetimes.

When you journal in a diary, you journal for yourself. When you journal on a scrapbook page, you invite others into your extraordinary world.

Michelle Pesce

Journaling Basics

Include the three components of scrapbook journaling

A well-journaled scrapbook page most often includes a title, primary information and a story. Those elements can be combined in a multitude of ways. They may be straightforward or quirky, lengthy or concise. The way they are handled depends upon the vision of the artist.

While journaling is a creative exercise, it should not cause your heart rate to soar or sweat to break out on your brow. Think of it as a walk down Memory Lane rather than an hour on the elliptical machine. Enjoy the sights, sounds and emotions during your journey. And make sure that you include the following on your scrapbook page so you will remember it forever.

The **title** on a scrapbook page is a "headline" designed to alert a viewer to the page topic. It conveys the mood of the artwork's subject through wording and design.

The **primary information** is the "who, what, when, where, why and how" portion of journaling. It provides "the facts, madame, just the facts" about the circumstances showcased on the scrapbook page.

The **story** is the meat of the journaling on a scrapbook page. The story captures the essence of the experience. It inserts humor or pathos as well as detailing thoughts and feelings.

Tia Bennett

THE IMPORTANCE OF HANDWRITTEN JOURNALING

While the wide offering of easily accessible fonts has caused many scrapbookers to turn to their computers when creating journaling, there remains something exceedingly personal about a handwritten message. Like a fingerprint, handwriting is distinct to an individual. The pressure of the pen, the slant of letters, the loops and swirls say a lot about the writer. And because preferred handwriting styles change societally with fashion, much can be surmised by analyzing the way passages were penned. You should strongly consider including handwritten journaling on your scrapbook pages to add that very personal touch.

TITLE

It attracts the reader and alerts her to the page subject. Manipulation of media and title placement contribute to the mood of the page.

Talon and Jonathan

First road trip in our new truck

Sightseeing in Buchart Gardens

Canadian Vacation

Autumn in the gardens is Gorgeous!

October 24, 2004

There is a special bond between Jonathan and Talon. I loved watching the two of them the day we went to Buchart Gardens on our Canadian Vacation. Hand in hand they skipped over the rock path that crossed the pond in the Japanese Garden. "Again!" Talon would beg. It didn't matter that Talon wanted to do it twenty times, Jonathan happily gave in to his request. I love watching those two together.

Samantha Walker

PRIMARY INFORMATION

It includes names, dates, locations and events. This helpful information concisely puts the page in context, ensuring that those who view it will understand and relate to the artwork.

STORYTELLING

It imparts emotion and imagery, engaging the reader and providing "the rest of the story."

Titles That Tempt

A good title is active and imaginative. It informs the viewer of the page topic and sets the mood for the artwork. A good title entices the reader to invest herself in studying the page.

Conceiving a strong page title takes focus. Begin by looking at your photos and reflecting on the occasion on which they were shot. Then close your eyes and allow yourself to become immersed in the essence of the event. When ready, write a single sentence that captures that essence. Free associate, writing down keywords that seem related. Pull out a thesaurus and create a list of connective words. Mix and match the words until something snappy materializes.

Marla Kress

Focus

This title drives home the astonishing ability of the young child to become immersed in his play. By running the title across the photo, the artist draws the viewer into the scene to enjoy an up-close look at the scenario.

Martha Crowther

Got Face

This title derives its cleverness from a popular advertising campaign ("Got Milk?"). The word play supports the over-sized photo and the focus of the layout.

TITLE RESOURCES

Sometimes dreaming up a perfect title feels as difficult as pulling a rabbit from a hat. When you keep coming up empty-handed, reach for these helpful sources.

Dictionary.com an online dictionary and writing resource

Lyrics.astraweb.com an archive of lyrics, searchable by artist and topic

Popcultmag.com a well-organized and kitschy look at lasting pop-culture elements

Quoteland.com a guide to famous quotes from celebrities and literature

Thesaurus.com an online guide to synonyms and antonyms as well as links to encyclopedia entries, word of the day and word translator

Worldwidewords.com a collection of unusual words and their history

Pull Together Primary Information

When creating your scrapbook page, you will almost always want to begin journaling with "The Five W's"—Who, What, When, Where, Why. This information is important in order to fully understand why the scrapbook page is being made.

Gather insights from others to include as part of your primary information. You may wish to ask the subject of your page to answer "The Five W's" rather than answering them yourself. If you discover that your subject is feeling chatty, why not throw in the "H" question—How? How does he feel about the occasion or experience? (You might even ask him how he feels about being asked all these questions, but be prepared to edit the response!) Once you have gathered primary information, you can use it in a variety of ways to support your design concept.

One of the best nights out in Durham, NH? Hands down, Wild 'N Wooly Night. The hostess is never certain how many women there will be, maybe 3, maybe 23, all settling into her living room, into the dining room chairs and the kids' beanbags that are brought in as the crowd grows. While the guest count may not be certain, what is certain is that there will be wool, cookies, cheeses, wine, bubbly water, and companionship.

Especially wonderful for me about Wild 'N Wooly nights is that they have given me the opportunity to spend time with women I probably would not have otherwise gotten to know. We would have smiled and said hi at the soccer field or the Durham Market, but we wouldn't have known all the little details about each other that we do now, that give us such comfort together.

Wild 'N Wooly conversations can cover sock yarn, felting, work, books our children are reading, our husbands' collective behavior around light [...], health, hom[...]

Deborah Hodge

Wild 'n' Wooly

This page, focusing on the experiences of a knitting group, includes many pertinent details. The artist writes about the ritual of gathering with the group, when and where they meet, and what goes on during the knit sessions. The enlarged image of the knitting supplies tells the story while the candid image of the group captures the emotion.

Shannon Taylor

Storytelling Festival

The journaling on this page concisely shares a memory in less than 200 words. The artist diligently explained the who, the what, the where, the when, the why and the how surrounding this storytelling festival.

THE FIVE "W'S"

W #1 Who: Who are the people in the photos? What are their names? (Make sure they are spelled correctly.) How are they related? Who was at the event but doesn't appear in the photos? Who took the photos?

W #2 What: What was the occasion, and what was happening at the moment that the photos were taken? What happened before and after the photos were taken?

W #3 When: When did this occasion occur (the exact date that the photos were taken)? When was the last time that a similar event took place?

W #4 Where: Where did the occasion take place? What country, state, region, area of town, building or home?

W #5 Why: Why is the event important? Why were these people attending the event? Why were these particular photos selected for the scrapbook page?

Keys to Compelling Storytelling

Your scrapbook is your story and should be told in a way that resonates with your own personality. It is not necessary to "find your voice" as a writer if you simply write in the same manner in which you speak.

While professionals often create an outline to help them with the structure of their writing, it is usually unnecessary when journaling. Your journaled story needn't follow along a tidy straight line. In fact, you may stoke your creativity by writing thoughts along a diagonal or in a spiraling circle. The most important aspect of scrapbook storytelling is the honesty and emotion driving the words. Express yourself!

Sometimes when you least expect it, you'll catch a glimpse of yourself. Do you see what I see? I'm sure you don't have any idea how much you have grown and changed. I suspect that you don't yet know what adorable big brown eyes you have and how they have that special spark when you think you are being funny. You don't see the way the light bounces off your hair or realize that the curly locks you once had are now gone. You certainly couldn't have any idea of how cute you look when you are running or how beautiful you are when you're sleeping. Jared, you are a busy little boy. You are very curious and seem to be able to get into more than I could ever anticipate. Most of the time you are so busy moving and doing that it is all I can do to keep up to you. But, like a reflection in a window, once in a while I catch a fleeting glimpse of who you really are. You are so much more than I even know right now, but I do know that you are kind and loving and that you have a wonderful sense of humor. I hope that when you see your reflection that somehow you will understand just how amazing you truly are!

Lonni McMullen

I'm sure you don't have any idea how much you have grown and changed. I suspect that you don't yet know what adorable big brown eyes you have and how they have that special spark when you think you are being funny. You don't see the way the light bounces off your hair or realize that the curly locks you once had are now gone.

Lonni McMullen

INSPIRATION TIPS

Bring your imagination to your inspiration starting line. Get ready. Get set. Go!

Get Ready Buy an inspiration journal. This is an idea collection plate. Fill it with scribbled musings, words, quotes and doodles.

Get Set Sit quietly with your journal and pen handy. Meditate on your memories. Play music, if you wish. Jot down ideas as they rise to the surface.

Go! Begin writing. Don't stop to correct your grammar or spelling. Simply let the words flow from your fingers to your paper. There will be time later to edit your work.

…About a month later, you were asking me about marriage again. You wanted to know if you could marry the kitties! I said, 'No, you can't marry kitties, silly!' Then I asked you if you wanted to marry Lily. You corrected me, saying that Lily was your best friend. 'Oh, then who do you want to marry?' You answered, 'Jessica!' I was curious. 'Why do you want to marry Jessica?' You answered, 'Because she has expensive train tracks!' I laughed out loud! What is even more funny is that Jessica doesn't have expensive train tracks. It's Lily that has them!

Mimi Schramm

Mimi Schramm

WRITING TIPS

Your storytelling voice should be uniquely your own, but it can speak more powerfully if you keep a few tricks in mind.

- Use lively verbs and descriptive adjectives.

- Show (be descriptive); don't tell (simply state the facts).

- Read your writing aloud and revise portions that don't roll easily off the tongue.

- Avoid run-on sentences, mixed metaphors and clichés.

- Practice word economy by avoiding redundancy and editing out extraneous verbiage.

The Uniqueness of a Personality

Explore your subject's special nature

There are many stories to be told, but the story of a unique personality (and doesn't everyone have one?!) is a tale that never grows old. Create scrapbook pages that call out the special traits of someone you love. Focus on the physical attributes of your subject, or perhaps her talents, goals, successes or interests.

Samuel Cole

Who's That Girl?

Short, descriptive captions about the model's favorite things were trimmed into strips and tucked into a pocket on this page. This journaling technique proves that text does not have to be long and elaborate to be informative and unique.

APT DESCRIPTIONS

When journaling about another, it is tempting to take the easy path and write only about the obvious: hair color, grade in school, favorite foods, favorite toy. But for more interesting storytelling why not explore topics that are a bit more...telling?

- How would she handle a rainy day?

- What would she do if she won a million dollars?

- What is one thing she couldn't live without?

- What does "the thing living beneath the bed" look like?

- If she could have lived in any other time in history, when would it have been and why?

- If she could fly, read minds, walk on water, or be invisible, which would she choose and why?

- If she could have lunch with one celebrity, whom would she select?

- What is the nastiest thing she's ever eaten? (You get the idea!)

All About...

The paragraph on the left side of this page gives the reader a little character development. It describes the quirks of the young girl in the photo. On the right side of the page, the artist hand wrote the girl's true favorites onto miniature tags and adhered them to a strip of distressed corrugated cardstock with brads.

Ashley Calder

Usually when you are asked about favorites, you just say 'everything!' And you really do love most everything…You are very nearly obsessed with certain books and videos, often recounting the entire story in amazing detail. Sometimes just the briefest mention of a word can set you off on an excited rave, as you tell us all about whatever your current favorite topic might be. Baby, I love your enthusiasm!

Ashley Calder

1. Why are those shoes called flip flops?
2. Why does the moon make waves?
3. Why do worms live in apples?
4. Why when pigs die it makes pork chops?
5. Why does luna follow me wherever I go?
6. Why did GOD put eyeballs in me?
7. Why do pirates have a patch on one eye?
8. Why is Arizona the Desert?
9. Why is marshmallow gushy?
10. Why do cactus have pokey things?

May- June 05

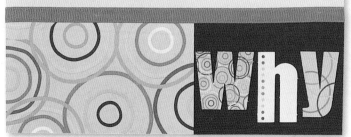

Monica Anderson

Why?

True dialogue imparts personality and keeps a memory in the context of a moment. Use dialogue to forever remember your child's young logic or your father's wisecracks. It helps to keep a small portable journal in your purse to capture these off-the-cuff remarks.

Your Innermost Feelings

Unlock your soul for journaling driven by emotion

It isn't always easy to look inside ourselves. Perhaps that is one reason why we tend to scrapbook about others. But writing about what goes on inside our own heads and hearts can help us understand our choices. It can lead to celebration when we have chosen well, and growth when we have stumbled. It can detail the experiences we have and the way we react to them.

Nic Howard

Growing Up

This personal journaling reads like a diary entry from the artist. She relates the moment of her son losing his first tooth to the moment he cut his first tooth as a baby. When trying to journal deeper thoughts, it helps to focus on a moment or part of a memory.

> *Jacob lost his first tooth today. He came home from school and handed me this tiny wee tooth wrapped in a piece of school toilet paper, and he just grinned. He was so proud. After hugs and cuddles and lots of 'I'm so proud' words from me, he flitted off somewhere and I just sat on the floor and stared at the tooth...I remember being SO PROUD when he cut that tooth as a baby...him sitting in his highchair and me tap tap tapping his gums with a teaspoon. Hearing the clink of a tooth cutting the first time was one of the most proud moments of my life. And there it was sitting in my hand...*

Nic Howard

to *listen* to God instead of just telling Him what I want
to sit and play Lego without watching the clock
to stop doing my own thing long enough to make popsicle stick swords and playdough sculptures for the kids
to love the colour red
to say "NO" to babysitting sometimes
to scrapbook the Moments, not just the events
to take naps when I can get them
to eat when I'm hungry and not when I'm not
to use up my stash
to creatively sneak vegetables into my meals
to lift with my legs, not my back
to see me as God sees me and others as God sees them
to praise my kids first and correct them second
to enjoy helpers in the kitchen and ignore eggshells in the cookies
to be content and thankful for all around me

Cathy (me) Sept. '05

THE journey

I'm learning to anticipate supper coming and make a plan for it

I'm learning to have an attitude of mercy and grace

I'm learning to play golf

I'm learning to scrapbook about myself, not just my kids

Cathy Schellenberg

I'm Learning

This page contains two excellent ideas for getting the journaling juices flowing. First, the artist focused on the topic of "lessons being learned" to direct her thoughts. Second, she formatted the journaling into a simple, unintimidating list.

IT'S ALL ABOUT YOU

It is often easiest to begin writing when you start with a list. Consider creating lists that delve into interesting questions.

- List 10 lessons you have learned since you had your first child.
- List 10 things you wish to do in this lifetime.
- List your favorite 10 movies and books.
- List your five earliest childhood memories.
- List the 10 best gifts you have ever received.
- List five professions you might have embraced (and the reasons you didn't).
- List the five scariest things on earth.
- List the television shows on which you would like to appear.
- List the five places where you'd most like to vacation.

Your Love and Passion

Share the things that make your heart flutter

Love can be so intense that you may feel words can't describe it. Yet poets and songwriters throughout the centuries have searched inside themselves and surfaced with thousands upon thousands of ways to express this wonderful human emotion. If they can do it, so can you!

Pamela Frye Hauer

Kids at Heart

The title of this page says it all. The journaling describes the beginning of the relationship—two young adults just barely old enough to vote and drink alcohol—to the present—two adults just cresting 30.

LOVE NOTES

There is a reason why love-struck people keep a photo of the one closest to their heart, close to their hands. Focusing on the photo opens up the floodgates of emotion and can lead to terrific journaling. Other keys to opening emotional pathways include:

- Listening to favorite love songs
- Reading favorite love poems
- Digging up and reading old love letters
- Watching romantic movies
- Talking to your parents about their courtship
- Telling someone about the story of your first meeting
- Reviewing memorabilia from your wedding or shared occasions
- Polishing jewelry or other gifts you received from your soul mate

He Loves Her; She Loves Him

Take a moment to appreciate all the little things you and your significant other do for each other. Now write them down and use them as scrapbook journaling. This is a wonderful way to show that you don't take each other for granted.

Erikia Ghumm

IN THE MOOD

We asked ourselves, "What are the most romantic songs, movies and poems of our time?" Well, the votes have been cast, the ballots counted and the results in! So when looking for some inspiration for those love-themed scrapbook pages, we suggest the following:

Favorite Love Poems
"The Invitation" by Oriah Mountain Dreamer
Sonnet 130, "My Mistress' Eyes Are Nothing Like the Sun" by William Shakespeare
"Beautiful Dreamer" by Stephen Foster
"Somewhere I Have Never Traveled, Gladly Beyond" by e. e. cummings
"Love's Philosophy" by Percy Bysshe Shelley

Favorite Romantic Movies
Breakfast at Tiffany's (1961, directed by Blake Edwards, screenplay by George Axelrod, based on the novel by Truman Capote)
The Princess Bride (1987, directed by Rob Reiner, book and screenplay by William Goldman)
When Harry Met Sally (1989, directed by Rob Reiner, written by Nora Ephron)
Say Anything (1989, written and directed by Cameron Crowe)

Favorite Love Songs
"The Luckiest" Ben Folds
"I Will Always Love You" Dolly Parton
"In My Life" The Beatles
"The Way You Look Tonight" Dorothy Fields and Jerome Kern
"Your Song" Elton John
"You Are Always on My Mind" Elvis Presley
"Unforgettable" Nat "King" Cole
"Wonderful Tonight" Eric Clapton
"You Are So Beautiful" Joe Cocker
"Crazy" Willy Nelson
"We've Only Just Begun" Paul Williams
"To Make You Feel My Love" Bob Dylan
"Time in a Bottle" Jim Croce
"Wicked Game" Chris Isaak
"Being with You" Smokey Robinson

The Dynamics of a Special Bond

Dissect the layers of love between people

Loving relationships are all about trust. We make ourselves vulnerable. They make themselves vulnerable. And with mutual respect, we approach, knowing that we are safe in each other's presence. Scrapbook pages that honor the bond between friends, siblings, parents and children explore these trusting and very important relationships—these enduring friendships.

Becky Thackston

Father

Journaling about a loved one can begin with a simple list of words. Consider all of the admirable characteristics he or she possesses. Either pepper a layout with those words, or do as this artist did: Use them as keywords to highlight and expand upon within a journaling block.

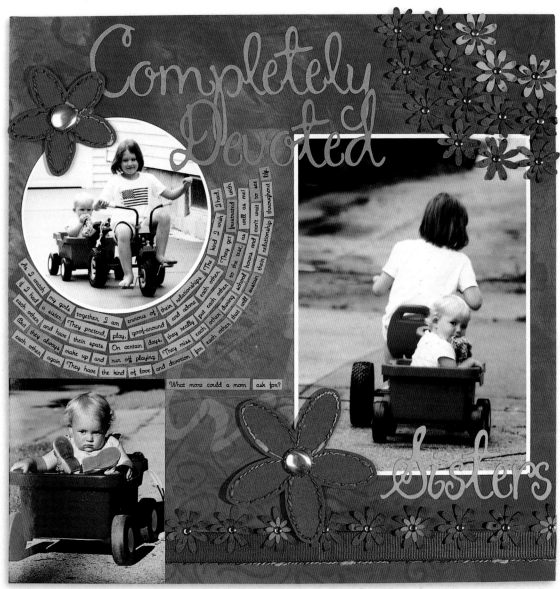

Heidi Schueller

Completely Devoted

Siblings share a dynamic bond like no other. One minute they are pulling each other's hair out over a squirt gun, and the next they are cuddling on the couch while watching television. Celebrate this bond with words that describe how the siblings are both alike and different. How does the older sibling protect and teach the younger? How does the younger sibling emulate the elder? How do they enjoy time together?

FRIENDS FOREVER

Friendships may ignite at first sight or kindle slowly and grow more intense over the years. No matter how they develop, they wrap us in love and keep us warm. Without our friends, we'd be…

- without emergency babysitters.
- sharing the good news with no one.
- having trouble realizing our inner and outer beauty.
- relying on the television to ease our loneliness.
- without chocolate after a bad day.
- still dating the wrong person.
- trying to squeeze size-8 hips into size-6 pants in the name of clearance.
- trying to shoulder the burden of our entire family's stresses.
- without a shoulder to cry on.
- still thinking it was all our fault.
- without the encouragement to take a chance.
- shopping alone.
- workaholics.

Pride in a Challenge Met

Honor hardwork and accomplishments

Challenges are a part of life. Facing those challenges with courage and fortitude is truly heroic, and heroes deserve to be recognized. Journaling about the struggles you and others have encountered and the way they were surmounted can help mend wounds.

Mary Rogers

Mad About You

The journaling on this page takes shape as a letter from mother to child. It details the struggles both have shared and overcome while dealing with the daughter's autism. Using a letter format for personal journaling helps ease the flow of emotion from pen to page.

" *...I will continue to focus on who you are and who you are able to become. I am so happy to have you in my life and thankful for the one constant in our relationship, the love that you have for your dad, Hayden and I. Your giggles are truly cherished moments. Madison, you are such a loving child, your smiles and kisses are cherished by us all, even when days go by without one.* "

Mary Rogers

Cherie Ward

The youngsters that have walked in and out of my classroom door though the years have persevered through poverty, neglect, abuse, incarcerated parents, domestic violence, indifference, cruelty, drug abuse, alcoholism, and many other social ills. Yet, somehow, the majority of these children come to school each day ready and willing to learn and to make school a happy place. This is the perseverance which I have learned to appreciate in a way I never would have, if it were not for these youngsters.

Cherie Ward

Perservering Life

The theme of perseverance runs thick on this page. For the journaling, the artist meditated on the struggles and tenacity of her students, which made her realize how strong and, hence, persevering these children are. Try organizing your own journaling around one theme for logical, clear and meaningful prose.

MAKING A DIFFERENCE WITH SCRAPBOOKING

Scrapbooking can help you recover from a loss, but around the country organizations are proving that scrapbooking can also be used to raise both money and awareness for worthy causes.

The Picture ME Foundation In 1998, Heidi Lewis created the Picture ME Foundation, an organization to help children with disabilities and serious illness through therapeutic scrapbooking and photography. Today the organization consults with hospitals and institutions about the benefits of scrapbooking for special-needs children. **pictureme.org**

Charity Crop Challenge, In 2003, Hilary Kraft lost her father, Bernie Kraft, to ALS (Lou Gehrig's disease). Bernie was a co-founder of Sticker Planet, a family-owned retailer of stickers and papers. As a response to her loss, Hilary organized the Charity Crop Challenge to raise money for research and patient-care funding. Participants are challenged to organize their own local charity crops (Sticker Planet provides prizes). In 2005, the challenge raised almost $20,000, all of which was donated to charities dedicated to fighting ALS. **stickerplanet.com**

More Great Journaling Ideas

Design your page style to support a creative journaling concept

Go out of your way to explore creative journaling ideas that will help define the look of your layout. Stretch the boundaries of clever. Here are some terrific concepts (and terrific pages) that might spur your imagination and give you the confidence to design your own page based on a journaling style.

You are only three years old and you've never been with anyone but your family. Some classmates had been in day care or with babysitters. But for you, being alone in school was quite a shock.

You love learning and activities, so we know how much school will come to mean to you. But what a bittersweet day it was for us all as you took that first big step toward independence.

Even when you forget to miss us, we will be still be thinking of you. And should you feel a little homesick, remember the kissing hand, little beast. Just press your hand to your cheek and remember, "Mama loves me, Daddy loves me."

Love always, Mama & Daddy

Aug. 31, 2004

Dear Stasiu,

Mama and Daddy never knew how hard it would be to send you off to school. We felt lost as our little boy took his big pack and followed his class up the stairs into St. Paul of the Cross.

Then it broke our hearts when we realized how hard your first day had been. You'd cried through the afternoon, saying that you missed your mommy.

You didn't know it but daddy and I stayed within a block's walk of the school the whole time, clutching our cell phone "just in case," drinking coffee and wondering if we'd made a mistake. We were missing you more than you were missing us!

Ann Hetzel Gunkel

PAPERS WORTH SAVING

Paperwork. It seems to collect everywhere—on our desktops, counters and bed stands! Instead of piling, tossing or filing interesting correspondence, display it in albums. Consider scrapbooking the following:

- Letters to Santa
- Letters to and from a favorite grandparent or relative
- Birthday invitations from a special friend (Get a photo of the friend to go along with the card.)
- Sticky notes and calendar entries
- That little note you find in a pants pocket
- Poems or papers written in school
- Letters of commendation, such as acceptance to a prestigious society or sports team
- Acceptance letters to colleges/universities
- Love letters
- Postcards and funny notes from friends
- E-mail correspondence

A Letter to a Loved One

Expressing strong emotions can be easier when you put your thoughts in a letter format. The "First Day of Preschool" layout includes a note penned by the artist to her son. It describes the struggle she and her husband felt on their child's first day of school.

A List of Important Highlights

Including a year's worth of information on one scrapbook page is easy when it is presented as a list. The artist lists the milestones and achievements her son experienced during his fifth year of life. Lists can be formatted into paragraphs or presented as bulleted information. For a creative visual effect, trim descriptions into captions and use them as a decorative photo frame or page border.

Martha Crowther

Lessons Explained

Lists of lessons learned show how far we've come. This page spins a humorous yarn on lessons, using them as a vehicle to detail the behaviors of the family dog.

Judith Mara

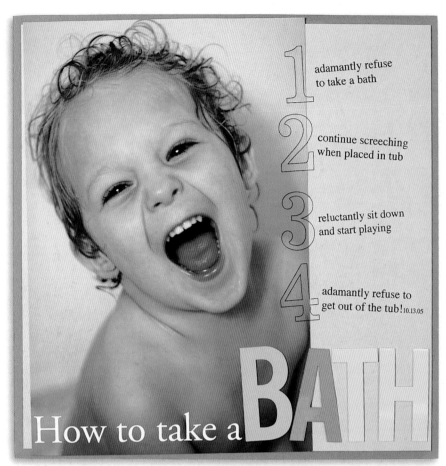

1 adamantly refuse to take a bath

2 continue screeching when placed in tub

3 reluctantly sit down and start playing

4 adamantly refuse to get out of the tub! 10.13.05

How to take a BATH

Joanna Bolick

How-to Instructions

Re-creating this journaling idea is as easy as 1, 2, 3. Break down any memory into a logical progression and write it as if you were giving someone a recipe.

Weather Report

Journaling is anything but predictable when it's given the touch of a weather forecaster. This fun treatment is easy to apply to most any memory. Chance of smiles: 100 percent.

5 day forecast:

Mostly puzzles with scattered breaks for meals and rest. We couldn't drag you away from your first 100-piece "big boy" puzzle!

July 2005

Chance of smiles: 100%

Susan Cyrus

C2 Weekend Flash   August 10, 2005

Father and son take birthday flight 3000 feet over Texas coast

Rachel Allen
Daily Planet Staff Writer

FRIENDSWOOD, TX - Saturday's skies looked hazy in the morning hours when local father and son Scott and Caleb Head were blessed with a rare birthday opportunity. But the weather cleared and sunny skies prevailed as Caleb Head, celebrating his 11th birthday with relatives, was asked if he would like to go flying. Caleb's uncle, Luis Yoffe of Dallas, Texas, generously offered his young nephew a birthday treat that few kids dream about, much less have the chance to experience.

"When Uncle Luis asked me if I wanted to go flying, I was excited and couldn't wait. I didn't know what to expect" said Caleb.

Caleb, his father Scott M. Head, and his grandfather Terry Humphrey accompanied Yoffe to Ellington Field, Houston, where Mr. Yoffe's private aircraft was waiting.

"I was a little worried how Caleb would manage flying in such a tiny little aircraft," said father Scott Head, "but we were all excited and would have never considerd passing up this

opportunity. I was really excited for my son, you could see the wide-eyed joy on his face as we walked out on the tarmac."

Leaving the airport in the Diamondstar composite 4-seat aircraft, the group took a sightseeing tour along Galveston Bay and the coast.

"We were looking for landmarks we could identify, we saw the restaurant we would be eating at later that day and wished we could just land there since the drive and parking issues are rather challenging." said Scott.

"I remember going over the water, all the little boats looked like little tiny sailboats in a bathtub because we were so high up" Caleb said. "We saw things that looked a lot different from up there, some lakes look square and roads looked like little threads"

After flying for an hour, the group returned to Ellington with a birthday tale to share. "Not many kids get to fly in a small aircraft like that, we are grateful to Uncle Luis, this was a gift my son, an myself, will not forget."

Angie Head

Newspaper-style Journaling

Give readers the scoop with newspaper-style journaling. This text, written by the artist's husband, is written from the perspective of Rachel Allen, the "reporter" (a moniker for a story character used at bedtime). The journaling mimics the tone of a daily newspaper, recounting the events of the day.

+Q
a

May I use clippings from real newspapers or magazines on my scrapbook pages or does that infringe on copyrights?

You may scrapbook published materials on your personal pages as long as the artwork is not published or sold.

Understand the Mechanics of Successful Design

Make the pieces of a layout fit

Clothing designers. Set designers. Landscape designers. Scrapbook designers. What do they have in common? Whether working with fabric, wood, plants or paper, all use design concepts to create a final product that is aesthetically pleasing. They call on basic principles such as balance, flow and texture to determine the placement of elements in relation to each other. This relationship ultimately determines the mood of the finished product.

Scrapbookers use photos, embellishments and journaling blocks to build pages. The shapes, sizes, colors and placement of these elements result in layouts that are terrific or just so-so. While the magic of design may seem elusive, and maybe just a little bit scary, most of the principles can be easily taught. The more you work with them, the better you will become at determining what works and what doesn't and— more important—why.

Creating strong layouts calls for the courage to fail. Just remind yourself that layouts can be remade and that you learn something from every attempt. Eventually, you'll find yourself turning out successive successful blue-ribbon designs for all your photos.

i love you.—

Pals
Buddies
Best
friends

me &
you

Right now you are saying something that I love to hear… "You're my best friend." It comes out of the blue when you least expect it, almost as if you're overcome with so much joy you need to get it out. It's often followed by a hug and is very heartfelt. I'm not sure that you know exactly what a "best friend" is. I assume that it's a pal, buddy or someone you love. Whatever the meaning, it's something that I love to hear. And little guy, you're my best friend!

Marla Kress

" *Creativity is allowing yourself to make mistakes.*
Art is knowing which ones to keep. "
Scott Adams

Create Page Designs Based on a Grid
Learn how to organize page components for effective design

A successful design has flow, meaning all of the elements work or fit together for clear communication. Break down your page into components and then fit those components together. Good design is simply a puzzle waiting to be put together. To simplify page design, organize page components into blocks (photo/s, title, journaling, accents). Now, think of your page background as a grid that has four equal quadrants. Place the blocks onto the grid, moving them around until they balance each other. The resulting layout should provide a logical path for the eye to follow.

Amy Goldstein

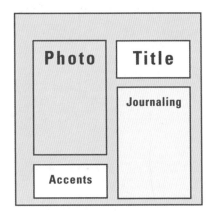

Use Clean Lines
Clean, straight lines are easiest for the budding scrapbook-page designer to work with. Their defining edges neatly contain elements and simplify design. This page relies on four simple, lineaer elements for a clean layout.

BREAK BAD DESIGN HABITS
Don't allow yourself to fall into design habits that make your layouts mundane!

- Do scrapbook pages you've created in the past rely on the same layout of elements? Avoid that design in the future.

- Do you tend to use the same colors and patterns on most of your layouts? Reach for seldom-used colors.

- Do you always print or crop your photos the same shape or size? Shake things up.

- After finishing a layout, hold it up to a mirror. The image will appear backward. This often reveals design flaws that easily can be corrected.

Divide the Design in Half

This layout is symmetrical, meaning that it consists of two equally-balanced halves. For no-fail symmetrical balance, mentally divide your layout in half and put the same size, shape and amount of page elements on each half.

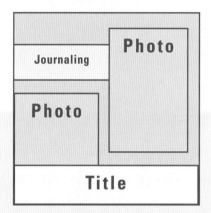

Laura Achilles

Overlap Elements

Overlapping page elements can create a sense of cohesion on a layout. On this page, the components are still treated as blocks of information. The artist achieved layout-design dynamite with this lovely layered effect.

Kelly Goree

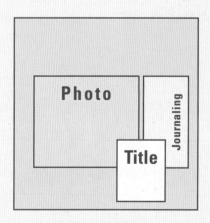

Emphasize a Superb Image

Use scale, proportion and other design techniques to draw the eye

Photos are the focus on a scrapbook page. The stronger the photo and its presentation, the stronger the art. Emotionally compelling photos featured in a large format usually guarantee a superb page. But the presentation of all photos can be strengthened with creative matting, cropping and framing.

Angela Biggley

Enlarge the Image

This enlarged and tightly cropped photo grabs immediate attention. The model appears lifelike as she occupies half of the page space.

+Q a

How do I choose a focal photo?

When choosing photos for a layout, spread out all of your potential photos on a large work surface. Allow your eyes to casually scan the images. You may find yourself stopping to take a closer look at a particular picture, or going back to view it again. More than likely, that picture should be your focal photo.

Linda Sobolewski

Use Interesting Frames

The sweet look on this model's face captures our attention, and the circular frame that wraps around her keeps it there. The frame is created by cutting an arching strip of patterned paper. The ends are then connected with a chain of paper flowers also cut from patterned paper.

> *Good art is not what it looks like, but what it does to us.*
>
> Roy Adzak

Apply Spot Color

To draw immediate and undivided attention to this beautiful boy's angelic face, the artist used spot color. The result is true blue, true blue eyes, that is, that stare into the distance and direct the viewer toward the whimsical journaling.

Laura Kockelkorn

DRAWING THE EYE

Contrast is a wonderful way to enhance a focal point and attract the eye. Try these ideas to create contrast on your scrapbook pages.

Contrasting mats An irregular-shaped mat will contrast against the straight edges of a photo and immediately draw the eye. Or, try a mat with stronger angles than the photo to create contrast.

Shape contrast If the shape of your photo contrasts against the shapes in the background, people will notice. If you background is linear, try cropping a photo to have a curved edge.

Color contrast Create drama with a black-and-white image on a vibrant background.

Energize Your Page with Color

Allow color to convey emotion

Color and emotion walk together hand in hand. Studies show that certain hot colors, such as red, actually speed up your heart rate and cool colors, like blue and green, are calming. When selecting a color palette for your scrapbook page, select colors that support not just the hues in your photos, but also the emotion and energy you wish to project.

This is my favorite part of our bedtime ritual: "I love you, Mommy. I love you, Sydney. I love you more. I love you more. No, I love you more. No, I love you more – more and more every day."

Diana Hudson

Cradle Tender Moments in Soft Color

This soft, muted color scheme of pink and blue whispers words of love. The softly feminine pink tones help warm the fair skin of the model while the blue adds a bit of contrast.

WHAT COLORS SAY TO US

Certain colors are associated with certain emotions. Use these associations when picking colors to reflect the correct mood for your pages.

Blue: sad, prayerful, restful, masculine, dependable
Red: angry, passionate, forceful, cautious, elegant
Orange: happy, ambitious, hungry, warm, creative

Green: envious, outdoorsy, hopeful, youthful, tranquil
Purple: powerful, omnipotent, holy, mystical, opulent
Pink: feminine, healthy, young, vibrant, romantic
Yellow: giddy, joyful, fresh, tart, refined
Black: exotic, dangerous, high-quality, scary, dominant
White: clean, new, airy, pure, empty, virginal

Shout Out with Vibrant Hues

The vibrant palette used on this page perfectly captures the excitement seen on the model's face in the focal photo. Hot pink is cooled down just a bit with soft orange and hints of green for a fun, summery combination.

Samuel Cole

Stay Calm with Cool Blues

Summery beach pages can be hot and vibrant, such as the one above, or cool, calm and collected, such as the one to the left. The gentle blues and greens of this page speak to a relaxing day at the beach, filled with sunbathing and treasure hunting.

Angelia Wigginton

Familiar Color Combinations

The colors combined on a layout affect and work with each other to create a bigger statement. The color wheel, a tool used by artists to help select color combinations, makes the task of pulling together a palette easier. Find one at most any hobby and craft store.

Samantha Walker

Create Energy with Contrast

Both these pages are created using a complementary color scheme. Complementary colors sit directly opposite one another on the color wheel. They work best when one color is used as the dominant shade and the other as an accent color.

Samantha Walker

+Q&a

I'm having a hard time picking colors to match my photos. What can I do?

An easy way to ensure the colors of your layout will match your photos is to convert your photos to black-and-white or sepia. This also is a great solution to working with photos with distracting backgrounds or loud, wild colors.

THE COLOR WHEEL

Use the color wheel to find color complements and exciting color combinations for your photos and papers. Most color wheels come with instructions that make using this handy device foolproof.

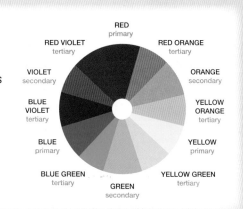

RED
primary

RED VIOLET
tertiary

RED ORANGE
tertiary

VIOLET
secondary

ORANGE
secondary

BLUE
VIOLET
tertiary

YELLOW
ORANGE
tertiary

BLUE
primary

YELLOW
primary

BLUE GREEN
tertiary

YELLOW GREEN
tertiary

GREEN
secondary

Color Intensity and Value

Color intensity, or the saturation level of a color, strongly affects mood. For example, a rich, bright red says "passion, heat, energy," while a cool pink shows red's gentler side. Saturation is determined by the amount of gray in a color. The more gray, the less saturated the color.

Color value is determined by how light or how dark a color is. Lighter color values are called "tints," and darker color values are called "shades." Those in between are called "midtones." Each value conveys a different mood.

Samantha Walker

Affect Mood with Color Intensity

These tags show varying degrees of color intensity. The less intense the colors, the softer the mood of the art. The winter tag is calm and relaxing with its soft palette. The spring tag is the most intense and shouts with energy. The summer tag tones down the cheery colors just a bit. The fall tag embraces the season with rich, warm levels of saturation.

TRIED-AND-TRUE COLOR FORMULAS

Monochromatic This palette is based on shade and tint variations of a single color.

Split-Complementary This scheme is formed by choosing a principle color and the two colors on either side of the principle color's complementary color.

Analogous An analogous combination is created by choosing two or more colors that are side by side on the color wheel.

Use Texture for Touchable Page Appeal

Add depth and enhance theme with tactile page elements

Texture can be brought to scrapbook pages with fabric, fibers and handmade and specialty papers. However, texture does not always have to be dimensional. Faux-texture, in the form of patterned paper, can bring the look of urban sidewalks and concrete, antiqued metal, wood paneling and age-old tile to your layouts. Sanding page elements or inking surfaces with textured tools such as bubble wrap or a natural sponge also provides that nubby, just-gotta-touch-it look.

Shannon Taylor

Lasso Rustic Textures

Every bit of texture on these two pages enhances the respective themes. On the "Cowboy" page, the frayed edge of the gingham fabric brings the bandanna around the model's neck to life. Cork and leather reflect the texture of the cowboy hat while the wooden frame has the rustic look of a split-rail fence on a dude ranch. Below, the crumpled, distressed and inky edges of the page elements perfectly mimics the rock formations and structures of the Grand Canyon.

What are some ideas for quick and easy texture?

Texture is easy to add. Try any of the following:

- Crumpled paper
- Ribbon, lace or trim borders
- Torn and curled paper edges
- Silk or paper flowers
- Cork photo mat
- Leather photo corners
- Jute-wrapped title letters

Leisa Tobler

Spring 2001

Aysha Cree

love

Imagine

child

The

Making

Of

A

DIVA

The heart can do anything.

Trudy Sigurdson

GREAT TEXTURES FOR GREAT PAGES

Add a touch of reality to your themed pages with the following texture ideas.

Baby chenille, terry cloth, bright and playful rubber lettering accents
Boy mesh, screen, burlap, denim, cork
Girl silk flowers, ribbon, soft velvet, glitter
Wedding velvet, tulle, satin, lace, pearly beads
Heritage leather, canvas, antiqued metal, tapestry
Seasons wood patterns, white bunting, shiny rubber, iridescent flakes
Pets braided nylon, leather, large eyelets, playful rubber accents
Holiday metallic sheeting, doilies, beads and baubles, glitter

Curtsy to Feminine Texture

The look of this page is lush and feminine. The silk flowers, lace, shiny brads and ornate patterns are the perfect way to costume a page about a little girl's love for playing dress-up.

Take Advantage of Simple Shapes

Finesse your pages with circles, squares and rectangles

When contemplating the perfect accent for your page, don't forget about the power of geometrics. Circles, squares and rectangles can be layered to create backgrounds, provide filler material for otherwise empty spaces, help direct the eye by becoming extensions of a photo and, with apt placement, balance a layout.

Marla Kress

My circle cutter isn't big enough to create a giant curve. What can I do?

Look for objects around your house to use as a tracing guide and then cut out the curve with a craft knife. Pots and pans, plates, laundry baskets and even the edge of a childhood favorite, the Sit 'n' Spin, will work.

Create Movement with Circles

Circle accents bounce like balls around this page. The artist created a bubbly border for the photo series with a collection of circles. They connect the photos and also help unify the page design by echoing the patterned paper. Punched-out journaling captions float like bubbles along the right side.

Balance with Squares

Squares and rectangles help balance the collection of photos on this page. Narrow rectangles anchor the meaty group of photos and blocks of patterned paper that stretch across the middle of the layout.

Debbie Hodge

Extend with Rectangles

What a clever concept! Thin rectangles placed on a diagonal look like photo extensions. The artist uses the strong diagonal line of the rail in the photo to inspire the design.

66

Art is the only way to run away without leaving home.

Twyla Tharp

99

Sue Fields

Move the Eye with Repetition

Repeat elements for a design that dances

Rhythm, expressed as a pattern of beats within a piece of music, moves a melody. On a scrapbook page, it helps guide the eye and unify a design. Within design, visual rhythm is created by repeating patterns, colors and shapes. You may wish to pull shapes or colors from those that appear within your photos. Soon, your pages will be marching to their own beat.

Christina Padilla

Repeat Shapes

The flower pattern found on the model's frilly costume inspired this artist to pepper the page with florals. Collections of knotted ribbon mimic flower shapes as does the mosaic pattern found in the paper. The large and small paper flowers are an obvious nod to the model's outfit.

MORE WAYS TO CREATE RHYTHM

Almost anything can be repeated to create a sense of rhythm on a scrapbook page. Try repeating any of the following:

- A singular photo
- A series of photos cropped to be the same size and shape
- A singular element, such as a sticker

- A singular shape in a variety of sizes and/or colors
- A series of similar shapes
- A combination of three colors
- Stamped images
- A series of tags
- Lines of various widths and lengths

Samuel Cole

Repeat Patterns

The circular shape of the sweet frozen treat inspired the artist to use polka-dot patterned paper in this design. The shape is repeated in the title with a font that features exaggerated curves. Small circle accents also help give the page a definite beat.

> *Everything in the universe has rhythm. Everything dances.*
>
> Maya Angelou

Repeat Colors

Color is a more abstract vehicle for rhythm creation. Here the color scheme is pulled from the model's red boating attire. A more muted version of the child's red hat is paired with colors that complement it beautifully. The palette is repeated throughout the color scheme of the layout with photo mats and corners, accent lines, buttons, the title lettering and a silk flower with a red center.

Sue Fields

Integrate Appropriate Type Styles

Strengthen layouts with just the right lettering

The lettering and text you use on your page is an integral part of design. A well-selected font coupled with thoughtful placement and sizing can have as big an effect on the mood of your page as color or texture. When selecting lettering and fonts, opt for styles that speak to the theme of the page. Use flowing fonts on pages that are gentle and romantic and more robust fonts on pages that are bold. Experiment with type sizes and interesting placements for best results.

Mix Type Styles

The repetition of the word "family" in a variety of fonts allows the eye to travel down a word ladder. The variety of font styles speaks to the different joys family life brings to this artist. The mix is energetic yet subtle enough not to distract from the portrait.

Sheredian Vickers

SELECTING THE RIGHT FONT

Thousands of fonts are only a mouse click away. Use these tips to choose the best one for your page.

Choose a font style to complement the mood of your page. Script styles are great for elegant and feminine pages. Block styles will complement masculine, sports or childhood pages. Funky fonts can add playful energy.

Use readable fonts for journaling. That super swirly font may impart the perfect mood for your page, but if it's hard to read, the journaling will not be appreciated. Try saving fun-but-hard-to-

read fonts for large titles. Consider highlighting key words when creating longer stretches of text.

Experiment with the placement of titles and text for dramatic effects. No one said journaling always needs to be in block form. If your page design features curving lines, try designing the journaling on subtle, waving baselines. Or, run a title vertically on a page for a change of pace.

Use Type to Balance

If the artist had placed this text elsewhere on the page, the large swath of background scenery in the photo would detract from the subject. Instead, the delicate font helps to balance the image while also imparting a sense of quiet serenity.

Pam Callaghan

Impact with Size

This large title helps draw the eye to the photo and helps balance the page. The large angular and distressed lettering works perfectly to complement the fun and exciting life of a teenager. The letters are stamped onto blue paper and then cut into funky block shapes that work well with the irregular geometric shapes in the background.

Samuel Cole

Relish the Craft

Experiment with popular scrapbooking techniques

Close your eyes. Picture your favorite photos. Allow your imagination to soar. Visualize those photos on exquisite scrapbook pages—stamped, inked, embossed, cradled by lush papers, embellished with beads, fibers or vintage ephemera. Now open your eyes and make your daydreams come true. In scrapbooking, as in dreams, there are no limits. With a basic understanding of scrapbooking techniques, you can make anything happen.

While all that is necessary to create an effective scrapbook are photos, paper, a pen, some adhesive and a trusty pair of scissors, you'll have even more fun if you invest in some additional tools and supplies. With those "extras" you'll open up all kinds of creative options. From sewing to stamping and from distressing techniques to mixing patterned papers, there is something to whet everyone's artistic appetite.

This is where you'll learn about the tools and supplies as well as dozens of techniques and pages ideas. Master the elementary skills and then stretch them and yourself to see how far you can go and grow.

Keep Laughing!

It's not very often that I capture true joy on Robby's face. He doesn't really enjoy having his picture taken. But on this day, he was lightly tossing pebbles at me and one made a basket in my shirt. He starting horse laughing! I just let him continue because his expression was priceless. Robby - July 2005

Shannon Taylor

> *Odd how the creative power at once brings the whole universe to order.*
>
> Virginia Woolf

Become Familiar with the Basic Supplies

A primer on the necessary equipment for a first-time scrapbooker

Scrapbooking allows you to live life, and then relive the joy of life, by recording your memories on scrapbook pages. In order to fully convey life's joys within your album, you will need the appropriate tools and supplies. What should you buy? How can you best use your new tools and supplies? Read on!

Choose the Right Album

Your album choice boils down to personal preference. Acid- and lignin-free albums come with either top- or side-loading page protectors—PVC-free plastic sheets to guard your scrapbook art against the elements. Top-loading page protectors open at the top and side-loading protectors open on the left side. Finished art is slipped inside the protectors.

4 TYPES OF ALBUM BINDINGS

Post-bound Two or three metal posts secure top-loading page protectors into the album. This type of binding can be expanded with post extenders. If you do not scrapbook in chronological order, inserting finished pages into post-bound albums can be challenging.

Spiral-bound A spiral coil binds pages to the album's spine and requires side-loading page protectors. Extra pages cannot be added to spiral-bound albums, nor can pages be removed. These albums are best used for gift or special theme albums.

Strap-hinge These albums come with pages that are bound by a plastic strap that slips through heavy-duty staples. Pages can be removed and added.

Three-ring Like a school binder, these albums use three D-shaped rings to hold top-loading page protectors. Pages can be easily added, removed or moved, but the wide binding leaves a gap between facing pages.

CSI: Scrapbooks

The investigation of irreplaceable photos left to rot in a magnetic photo album.

0800 hours: While cleaning out the attic, a mysterious box is found and a long-lost photo album is discovered. Upon further inspection, it is noted the photos had the misfortune of being placed in a magnetic photo album. These poor photos have been subjected to double jeopardy—they were stored in an attic wrought with extreme fluctuating temperatures, and they were being slowly eaten away by the unstable chemical conditions of the magnetic photo album.

0900 hours: Exhibit A (the photo album) is taken to the evidence room (the kitchen). There, a lab expert (Mom) carefully peels away the plastic sheeting covering the photos. She uses a thin knife blade to peel the corners of the photos from the offending adhesive. She works slowly and carefully, wedging the knife blade between the pictures and the sticky album. She successfully frees most, at times reaching for archival-quality adhesive remover to aid her mission.

1000 hours: The lab expert has reached an impasse. Some photos remain stuck to the plastic sheet, trapping them and threatening demise should they be forcefully removed.

1200 hours: The lab expert must think on her feet. Defeat? No way! She can either scan the photos and make prints to scrapbook, or take the album to a professional photo conservator, who will try to free the trapped, priceless photos.

Run credits—and be sure to credit our star, the savvy scrapbooker.

THE ART OF PRESERVING PHOTOS

Using only archival-quality materials and storing photos and memorabilia under optimum conditions will ensure the longevity of your memories.

What you'll need Be sure that any materials you use to organize and store your photos are of archival quality and have a neutral chemical composition (7.5 - 8.5 pH level). Paper should be acid- and lignin-free. Any plastics should be PVC-free and made of polypropylene or polyethylene.

Storage conditions Keep photos and memorabilia away from bright light and sunlight. Also, storage temperatures should be between 60-75 degrees Fahrenheit. Ideal humidity is between 20-50 percent. It also is important for temperature and humidity to remain stable.

Polaroids, negatives and memorabilia Store photos separately from Polaroids, negatives and memorabilia. Polaroids contain chemicals that can react with photos. Negatives also can react with photos, but it's also a good idea to keep negatives stored elsewhere in case of disaster. Memorabilia oftentimes is not created with archival-quality products. Spray memorabilia with acid-neutralizing spray or encase in photo-safe envelopes.

Stock Your Scraproom with the Right Stuff

There is a tool on the market designed to make any scrapbooking possibility a reality. Most techniques, however, require a few basic "must-haves." Start with these nifty devices and fill your toolbox as you get more excited about the craft. While shopping for tools, don't forget to cruise the aisles for papers, stickers and other fun embellishments.

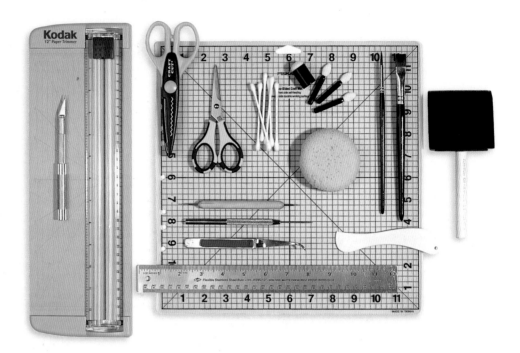

The Basic Tool Kit

Applicators Purchase a few paintbrushes of varying tips and textures to apply color and texture. Sponges work well with ink and paint to edge elements and add texture. Cotton swabs can be used to apply chalk and for detailed cleanup operations.

Trimmers Craft knives cut quick mats, create hand-cut titles and can be used with templates.

Scissors Dedicate a good pair of scissors to paper and another for fabric. Scissors with decorative edges (such as pinking shears) also are handy. Invest in a good paper trimmer for long, straight cuts.

Stylus This round-tipped tool is designed for dry embossing, but it also comes in handy for outlining areas for cutting and adding quick texture.

Tweezers They are an extension of your hand when the job is too hot to handle or too small to grasp.

Paper piercer A necessity for setting eyelets and brads, this tool can be used to create a guide for hand-stitching.

Bone folder Use this tool to score folds, indent paper and brandish images.

Self-healing cutting mat This will keep your work surface clean and safe. Gridded mats make measuring and cutting photo mats much easier.

Cork-backed metal-edged ruler The sturdy metal edge ensures clean cuts while the cork backing prevents slippage.

WHAT'S INSIDE HIS TOOLBOX?

Your best scrapbooking tool for a certain job may be found in that toolbox in your garage. Take a look.

Sandpaper Nothing works better to roughen a page. Use it on paper or (duplicate) photos. Rub it horizontally and vertically for a cross-hatch design.

Hot glue gun If you're into metal, hot glue may prove stronger than other adhesives.

Fishing line This thin, clear, strong fiber is perfect for stringing beads and charms.

Hinges The smaller varieties make great mechanisms for flip-up page elements.

Cork It's a wonderful texture to add to pages.

Awl It does what the paper piercer will not when working with leather or other thick materials.

Paper, Embellishments and Other Fun Supplies

The proverbial candy in the candy store—that's exactly what papers and accents are to a scrapbooker. For this very reason, the scrapbook store can be dangerous place for pocket-books. When shopping for supplies, it's a good idea to shop with a list and a budget. Avoid the temptation to buy everything you love—stick to consumable supplies that you know you will use. But don't be too rigid...have fun and experiment with a few items you've never used before.

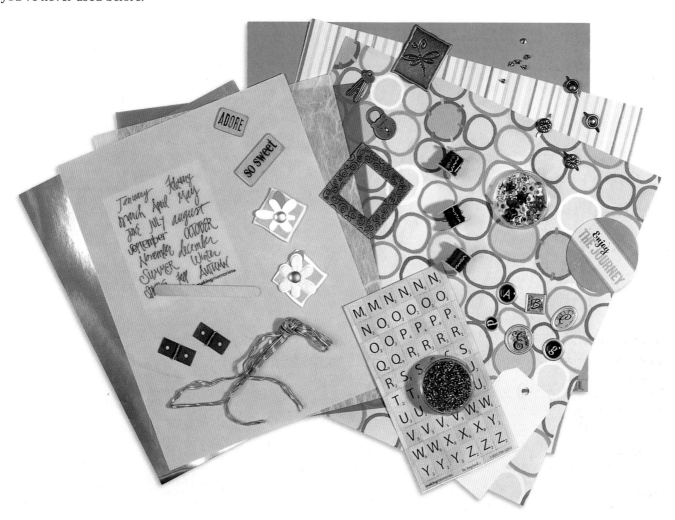

THE WIDE WORLD OF PAPER

Acid- and lignin-free paper, in all its varieties, is the essence of scrapbooking. Here is a brief overview of some popular papers.

Cardstock This sturdy paper can be used for backgrounds, photo mats and paper accents. It is available in almost every color imaginable. Textured varieties also are popular. Also look for double-sided cardstock.

Patterned paper This decorative paper is approximately half the weight of cardstock, but can be used similarly. A pattern exists for every scrapbookable occasion.

Vellum This semitranslucent paper is perfect for layering and for journaling. It is available in a wide range of colors. Patterned and textured vellums are available, as is self-adhesive vellum.

Fabric paper Faux fabric papers have the stability and texture of fabric but can be manipulated like paper.

Metallic paper These shiny sheets add lightweight texture and shine to pages. They can be stamped, embossed and texturized for unique looks.

Specialty paper These include everything from handmade papers to those made of natural botanicals. While patterns, textures and colors offer rich creative possibilities, the archival quality of these papers cannot be guaranteed.

Get Inventive with Your Photos
Simple ways to enhance your photos

Want a surefire way to create a scrapbook layout that stops viewers in their tracks? Focus on the photos. After all, they are the stars of the scrapbook page. Simple cropping techniques, creative options for printing photos and interesting photo techniques are just a sampling of ways to enhance stunning images.

Crop Photos for Emphasis

The phrase "to crop a photo" has a variety of meanings. At its most basic, it means to remove any unwanted parts of a photo such as a distracting background. At its most dramatic, it is any variety of techniques used to manipulate an image. Effective cropping enhances the value and lure of an image.

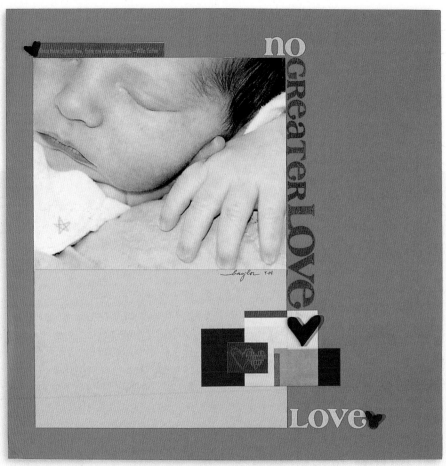

Tia Bennett

Remove Distracting Backgrounds

The layout features a cropped and enlarged photo of a precious sleeping baby. The artist felt the background of the photo distracted from the baby's adorable face, so she cropped in close, filling the frame with just the baby's face. She then converted the image to black-and-white to create a classic image and to downplay any remaining background.

How can I create mats that will make my photos pop?

Creating mats that contrast against the background will help draw attention to a photo. When looking at the photo, identify a secondary or tertiary color in the image. Use that hue for the mat. Then, pick a background color that creates a natural environment for the photo but also contrasts with the mat. A lighter photo mat on a darker background helps the photo pop.

Angie Head

Lengthen a Photo

This photo has been "stretched." This cropping technique emphasizes the photo subject while maintaining the details in the photo background. Simply cut the extraneous photo borders (top/bottom or sides) into slices and adhere, leaving a small gutter of space between each.

CROPPING TOOL

Whether you are going to personally crop your photos or have them professionally cropped and printed, "L" bars are great cropping tools. Cut two "L" shapes from sturdy cardstock and use them to create a window over your photo. Move them around, make the window bigger or smaller until you find the best crop. Mark crop marks with a grease pencil to guide yourself or the photo finisher.

Print Photos on Unexpected Surfaces

Add to a photo's beauty by choosing an interesting surface on which to print or transfer the image. Whether your goal is to create, for example, an ethereal or vintage appearance, there is sure to be a print surface that will support your concept.

Vellum

Printing a photo on vellum gives it a dreamy, atmospheric quality. This is a great technique for photos that are slightly blurry or appear washed out.

Transparency

Create a custom overlay by printing photos onto an inkjet transparency. Be sure to set printer preferences to "print on transparency."

Inkjet Paper

The best inkjet printers and inkjet paper produce superb images with a long archival life. Follow the manufacturer's recommendations for best results.

Watercolor Paper

Heavy, and high in cotton content, this paper says "fine art." Watercolor paper comes in a variety of surfaces from smooth to rough. This paper is ideal for rustic or highly textured layouts.

Fabric

Printing photos onto fabric, such as canvas, will result in a textured image. Try this technique with cream fabric and sepia prints for a vintage feel.

Photo: Joanna Bolick

What kind of printer do I need to re-create the above effects?

You'll want to use an inkjet printer for these types of projects. Inkjet printers create images from miniscule drops of ink. The absorption of these drops of wet ink are necessary for images to be printed on porous surfaces such as fabric. Select the "transparency" setting in your printing preferences menu, if applicable. Also, check the printer manual to find the maximum thickness of media your printer can handle.

Execute an Image Transfer

This technique involves transferring an image from photo paper to a transparent surface. The transparent image can then be overlaid onto backgrounds. Here, the artist laid a transfered image of a farm scene over a piece of ephemera.

Erikia Ghumm

CREATE A LAMINATE TRANSFER

There are many ways to execute an image transfer. Laminate transfers are one of the easiest and least toxic.

Make a color copy of the photo on a copier or print a color copy from a laser or inkjet printer using archival, water-proof ink. Remove a background from a laminate-transfer sheet and apply the copied image facedown onto the sticky side.

Reapply the backing sheet to the back-side of the laminated image. Use a bone folder to firmly burnish the sheet to the image.

Submerge and soak the sheet in luke-warm water for a minute. Remove and gently scrape away the white paper. Blot dry and adhere the image to layout.

Master Celebrated Scrapbooking Techniques

Browse this gallery of tried-and-true craft ideas

Scrapbooking is a limitless hobby because it includes an enormous range of creative possibilities. A blank scrapbook page equals a canvas suitable for any type of artist, whether she is a painter, a stamper or even a digital savant.

Stamping and Embossing

Stampers can create images, letters, patterns and texture with almost no tools at all. Simply ink the image on a stamp, press it to paper and...ta da...art! Thousands (if not millions) of stamp patterns exist. Each can be used time and again. When stamping a scrapbook page, it is preferable to use pigment ink. Clean your stamps well after every use and store them on shelves, in plastic storage bins, binders or shoe boxes.

Pamela Frye Hauer

Great Ways to Use a Stamp

Make the most of your investment by exploring all the ways stamps can be used.

- Create custom patterned paper with background, letter, number or image stamps.

- Stamp onto shrink plastic to create original charms or accents that appear acrylic.

- Stamp into polymer clay or heated embossing enamel to create impressions.

- Use a brayer to add a colorwash over a stamped image.

- Place a die-cut shape or letter onto a shadow stamp, ink and stamp to create a resist image.

STAMPS AND INKS, EXPLAINED

It is often difficult to sort fact from fiction and that includes craft facts. When it comes to stamping, there are all kinds of misunderstandings floating around. Now, for stamps and inks, we present "the rest of the story."

Types of stamps *Rubber stamps* are the most widely available and are made of durable, high-quality rubber.

Acrylic stamps are becoming more popular because of their transparent quality. The fact that the image and the mount are clear results in perfect placement. They are tougher to keep clean, though.

Foam stamps result in an image with a slightly distressed texture. They are not as durable as rubber or acrylic stamps, and work best when used with acrylic paint.

Mounted vs. Unmounted *Mounted stamps* come with the stamp image already adhered to a wooden handle, or mount.

They are long lasting and easy to use, but can present storage challenges. *Unmounted stamps* can be stored in binders. They peel on and off of acrylic mounts via static cling.

Stamping inks *Pigment ink* is preferable for scrapbooks. It is archival, waterproof, fade resistant and lightfast. It requires longer to dry. Speed up drying time by heat embossing (see steps on p. 109).

Dye inks dry very quickly. They produce subtle color and are great for shadow stamping.

Watermark ink is transparent or lightly tinted to create tone-on-tone effects or resist images.

Solvent ink is needed for stamping on nonporous surfaces such as metal or plastic.

Brush markers can be used to color directly onto a stamp or color in a stamped image.

Pamela Frye Hauer

STAMP AND HEAT EMBOSS

Heat embossing turns a stamped image into an image that is dimensional with a glossy finish. Embossing can be done on paper, metal and other embellishments. It is quick and fun to do.

Ink your stamp with pigment ink, being careful to evenly apply ink to the entire image. Apply ink to your stamp directly from the pad with a tapping motion.

Stamp the image onto your background using even pressure. Do not rock the stamp, which will cause your image to blur.

Immediately sprinkle embossing powder onto the wet image. Shake off excess powder into a tray and return it to its bottle.

Hold a heat gun a few inches away from your image and heat until the embossing powder becomes shiny.

Using Colorants

From simple shading to custom coloring paper and fabric, colorants can add splash and spark to any page. Experiment with them to create dimension or add additional definition to page accents. Use them directly on photos or to add a hint of color here and there. You'll be as happy as a child in art class. Guaranteed.

Fun and Easy Colorants

There is a wide range of colorants available to scrapbookers. Each has its own special quality and many are best used for particular tasks. Here's what you need to know about the most popular colorants around.

Colored pencils are a natural choice for shading images or coloring in stamped images. The more pressure you apply, the more saturated the color will be.

Metallic rub-ons look like a rich, shimmery, almost oily chalk. You can use them in much the same way that you use chalks to add definition or dimension.

Watercolor paint can be brushed, splattered or sprayed on to add soft color. Use it with stamped images or create your own background paper by releasing your inner artist.

Chalks are one of the easiest colorants to manipulate. They are the perfect choice for defining torn edges, enhancing the raised surface of embossed or crumpled paper and hand-tinting black-and-white or sepia photos. Apply with cotton swabs, makeup sponges or your finger. Spray chalks with a fixative to ensure the longevity of the color.

Acrylic paint helps achieve a distressed look. Use it to create a colorwashed background or to add color to metal, plastic, fabric and more. It is a great medium to use with foam stamps to produce an opaque, distressed image.

Colorants at Work

From the subtle shading to a rich colorwash, this page is alive with color. The artist employed several types of colorants to add depth and shading, emblazon bland chipboard letters, create a unique rendering, and more.

Acrylic Paint

is used to custom color chipboard letters in the title as well as chipboard squares in the top right corner.

Chalks

are used to enhance the floral design of embossed paper.

Samantha Walker

Colored Pencils

provide shading and detail to a stamped image on the journaling block.

Watercolor Paint

is used to create custom background paper in the lower right corner and to detail the journaling block.

Aging and Distressing

"Too new" can appear unapproachable and untouchable, while something that is love-worn tends to draw us in. Pages that have had aging and distressing techniques applied to them look as if they have lived a rich life of adventure. Their vintage appeal says, "I *have* been there, and I *have* done that, and I *deserve* to be passed down through the generations." Creating scrapbook pages with a heritage feel takes less time than you think.

Laura McKinley

Distress Cardboard, Tear Paper and Ink

The aging and distressing techniques used on this page perfectly capture the spirit of a rough-and-tumble boy. The distressed corrugated cardboard background creates wonderful texture to mimic the mountain of dirt being summited. Torn paper and walnut ink add to the delightfully messy and adventure-filled theme.

Laura McKinley

Crumple and Ink Paper, Distress Elements with Sandpaper

Crumpled and inked paper help this page say farewell to summer and hello to autumn. To match the wind-whipped theme of the page, the artist sanded some of the paper elements, including the envelope and the plaid paper mat.

Crumpling paper makes it bulky. What can I do to flatten it?

First, crumple paper and further distress as desired. With your hands, flatten the crumpled paper. Then, cover it with a cotton towel and smooth it with a warm iron (spritz paper with a little water first to really flatten it). Do not iron papers that are coated or have any flammable or heat-sensitive content.

Creating Paper Accents

Paper is the most used medium in scrapbooking. Beyond building a foundation for a scrapbook page, it can be called upon to create a cornucopia of paper accents—lightweight choices that won't overburden layouts. Look for papers that match your page theme in patterns, colors and textures. Have fun experimenting with papers of different weights and textures.

Wendy Chang

Punch a Pattern

Punch art is an easy way to create themed shapes or simple geometric shapes. Punches are incredibly versatile. They can be layered or embellished for very different effects. Here, the artist uses circle punches to create a scalloped edge and add detail to the geometric pattern of the background paper.

Piece Patterned Paper

Custom paper-pieced designs add personal flair to any project. Draw a pattern and trace pieces onto patterned paper. Cut out the shapes and piece them together.

How can I keep my paper punches sharp and clean?

Every so often, punch through aluminum foil to keep punch blades sharp. Remove any jammed paper with tweezers, and use adhesive remover to clean punches from sticky residue. To keep punches lubricated, punch through wax paper.

Wendy Chang

Plant a Flower

Large floral accents are stylish and provide fun design elements on pages. By curling the leaves of this paper flower and chalking the edges, the artist creates lifelike dimension.

Wendy Chang

CREATE A DECORATIVE FLOWER

It takes little time to make a floral embellishment that will add personality to your scrapbook page. Simply follow the steps below.

Use a template to cut the petals of a flower.

Lightly ink the edges of each petal. Curl the petals by wrapping them around a round-barreled pen.

Attach each petal in a circular pattern.

Embellish the center of the flower. Flip it over and add a piece of foam adhesive close to the top of each petal and adhere the flower to the background.

Making Things Stay Put

Adhesive or hardware? That's a choice you will make countless times when scrapbooking. Adhesive is strictly functional while hardware can put the "fun" in functional. Hardware, such as brads, clips, conchos, eyelets, hinges, photo turns and rivets, are great for adhering transparent items such as vellum or transparency overlays. If you are worried about adhesive showing through an element, opt for a fastener.

Sheila Doherty

Get Funky With Fasteners

Look beyond utility when working with clips, hinges, brads, and eyelets. Today's scrapbook fasteners come in an array of colors and a bouquet of decorative styles, making them a natural choice for creating fun patterns that draw the eye, balance a page or add creative zing.

STICKY SITUATIONS

Adhesive choices abound in scrapbooking. Here are some descriptions to help you choose the right one.

Clear-drying glue When you need a heavy-duty adhesive, wet glue gets the job done. It requires ample time to bond.

Glue stick This adhesive works beautifully for adhering large blocks of paper or photos to backgrounds.

Glue pen A glue pen will glide into hard-to-reach places.

Photo sticks This adhesive is actually sectioned tape great for adhering photos or small accents.

Photo tape This is unsectioned tape that can be custom cut to the desired length.

Tape roller Quick and easy, this versatile roller dispenses double-sided tape.

Double-sided tape sheets Clear tape, it is great for heavy-duty jobs or for adhering glitter, beads and baubles. It can be cut or punched into any shape.

Foam adhesive For added depth, use foam adhesive, available in various shapes and widths.

Go for Fashion and Functionality

All fasteners can be useful scrapbooking tools as well as fun design elements. On this page, brads were used to create fun squiggles while eyelets and paper clips secure the photo and journaling to the page in a colorful style.

Rebekah, Lucas and Tyler love to slide. It's the first thing they head to when we go to the park and the toy they spend the most time on while we're there. And it's not just sliding down that's fun, oh no. They like climbing up the slide too, and I don't mean the stairs. Everyone waits at the bottom for their turn to climb up and slide right back down, usually on their tummies. The real excitement comes when they all try to climb up at once and end up in a dog pile at the bottom.

sliding

Sheila Doherty

SET AN EYELET

Eyelets can bedevil a beginner scrapbooker, but in three easy steps, they set with ease.

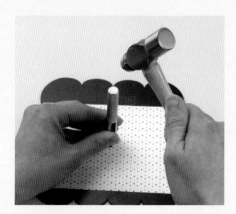

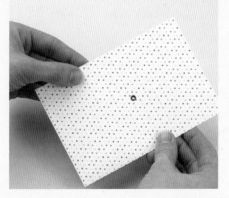

Using a paper piercer, punch a hole in the desired location.

Insert an eyelet into the hole and flip the paper over.

Insert the setting tip of your eyelet setter into the center of the eyelet and hit the end of the setter firmly several times with a hammer.

Making Things Fold, Flip and Pull

Audience participation, please. That is the motto of an interactive scrapbook page. Moving elements invite the reader to reach out and touch. For the scrapbooker, the elements create extra space on a layout on which to add more photos and journaling. Or, they provide nonchalant hiding places for more personal photos and journaling.

Wendy Chang

How can I customize a page protector to accommodate for moving or interactive parts?

Once you have finished the layout, create a cutting guide with paper that is the exact dimension of the interactive element on the page. Slip the page into a page protector and, using temporary adhesive, adhere the cutting guide to the protector in the necessary location. Remove the page from the protector and trim around three sides of the guide.

Fold an Accordion Card

An accordion-folded element consists of a series of neatly folded and stacked papers that cradle precious memories between peaks and valleys. Accordion elements can be bought premade or easily created by folding and reverse-folding a wide strip of paper. (Use a bone folder for neat, even folds.)

Flip a Photo Wall

The backside of flip-up elements is the perfect home for extra photos or journaling. Flip-up elements can be attached with hinges or adhesive.

All parents wish for their children to get along. We are lucky that not only do you get along, you are very much each other's best friends. You do everything together. When you experience a triumph, you want to share it with the other first. When you face fear or adversity, you look first to the other for comfort. And when you experience something new, you want to do it together, hand in hand. While we originally planned on having you farther apart, looking back, we would have it no other way. Only 23 months apart, but close enough that you can, and do, grow together, every step of the way. We are so grateful. We hope and pray that long after we are gone, you will still be best friends. Forever.

Wendy Chang

Pull a Journaling Block

Pull the tab and out slides journaled sentiments about this young child. The artist kept the left edge of the photo unadhered so she could slip a journaling block behind it.

reminisce /re-mu-'nis/ verb
1. to bring an image or idea from the past into the mind with fondness
2. to think or tell about past experiences

Wendy Chang

Pocketing Items for Safekeeping

Pockets are a wonderful way to keep page elements secure yet accessible. Pockets can hold extra photos, memorabilia, or keep personal journaling tucked away. Premade pockets are available, or you can create your own, making sure that you use sturdy paper and strong adhesive to connect it to your page. Don't overstuff your pockets. It's much better to add a few extra to your layout to hold additional items.

Amy Goldstein

Stitch a Pocket

This pocket holds cards, memorabilia and personal reflections from a 40th birthday party. The artist chose a vibrant patterned paper to match her mood and spirit and attached it to the page with a funky zigzag stitch.

Amy Goldstein

Create a Pocket Album

Mini albums can hold more than photos and journaling, as this one illustrates. Under the "Songs of the Heart" title is a pocket holding a CD of love songs for the charming couple. The artist covered paper CD sleeves with patterned paper and then bound them into an album.

PICK A PERFECT POCKET FOR YOUR PAGE

Pockets come in all shapes, sizes and materials. Which is the perfect pocket for your page?

- Fabric pockets are the sturdiest and, depending on the give of the fabric, can be quite filled. For best results, stitch a fabric pocket directly to your page.

- Paper pockets are easy to create. They can exist as traditional pockets or be folded into envelopes. Paper can be delicate, so refrain from filling this type of pocket with anything bulky or heavy.

- Transparency pockets allow viewers a peek at the contents.

- Plastic pockets can be purchased and are great for encapsulating memorabilia.

Amy Goldstein

Fold a Pocket

This handmade pocket is fashioned after a folding card. The folio closure keeps it cutely secure. It opens to reveal heartfelt journaling.

MAKE A SIMPLE POCKET

Page pockets can be extraordinarily elaborate or sweet and simple. Below are steps for creating a simple, folded pocket.

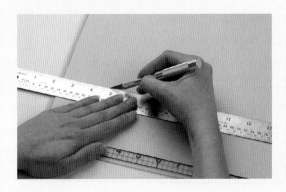

Trim a strip of paper to your desired size.

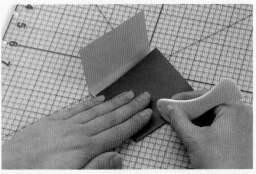

Fold the bottom edge of the strip up and the top edge down, scoring with a bone folder. Embellish as desired.

Creating Unique Backgrounds

It is not uncommon for new scrapbookers to develop paper addictions fed by rows upon rows of delicious patterned paper choices. Put your passion to constructive use by experimenting with different background designs. Photos resting atop a well-designed background often need little else in the way of accents. If you are new to mixing patterns, turn to coordinating lines of papers that provide guaranteed results.

In all things of 2005

nature

there is something of the marvelous

Sandy Minchuk

Mix Patterns

A coordinating line of orange and green papers make this layout a sure-fire winner. The muted orange background allows the vibrant tiger lily in the photo to take center stage.

MATCHMAKER TIPS FOR MIXING PATTERNS

Some couples are simply made for each other and a good matchmaker can point her finger and select those that will work best together. Consider these suggestions when doing your own matchmaking.

- Pick patterns that share the same base color. Papers with varying base colors will result in a muddy-looking layout.

- Opt for a mix of organic and geometric shapes. For example, mix florals with stripes.

- Vary the scale of the patterns—choose one pattern with large motifs and others with smaller motifs.

- Use the color wheel to help you pick complementary colors of patterned papers.

Color Blocking

Colorblocking means to use blocks of color to create a background. This page demonstrates successful colorblocking. The artist chose two colors of paper, based on the photo (pink and blue) as well as a contrast color. She then cut the colored papers into blocks and created a frame around the enlarged photo.

Diana Hudson

Pattern Blocking

Pattern blocking is a technique similar to color blocking, but uses patterned paper rather than solids. It results in visually interesting layouts (and is a great way to use up your paper scraps)!

Marla Kress

Tying Things Up and Tying Things Down

Scrapbookers eye an aisle of ribbon in a craft store with the intensity of a cat ready to pounce. Who can blame them? Ribbon comes in as many patterns and colors as patterned paper, and many product lines now include matching ribbon sets. Ribbon is an easy way to enhance the mood of a page because it is so very easy to use and so very versatile.

Samantha Walker

Lace Ribbon Through Eyelets

Laced ribbon adds texture, interesting pattern and movement to scrapbook pages. Here, the artist used the technique to connect two pieces of trimmed paper. She set eyelets along both sides of the paper pieces in which to lace the ribbon. She then laced up the paper pieces, crisscrossing the ribbon just as she would if she were lacing up a shoe.

+Q a

How do you print on ribbon?

Type your journaling and print it onto the paper. Using double-sided tape, adhere a strip of ribbon over the printed journaling. Re-insert paper into the printer and reprint. Remove the ribbon and adhere to your page.

Samantha Walker

Run Ribbon Across a Background

Who says the background of a scrapbook page must be made of paper? This page certainly demonstrates otherwise! The artist created her own highly textured and patterned background by running lengths of coordinating ribbons of various widths across a piece of cardstock. She used strips of double-sided adhesive to adhere the ribbon.

Frame a Page with Ribbon

When you're searching for that special finishing touch for a layout, reach for ribbon. Wrap it around your page to create a frame. This ribbon border softens the busy background pattern while echoing the model's striped shirt. The thick denim texture helps to visually confine the energy of the page.

Samantha Walker

Getting Friendly with Your Computer

Computer scrapbooking is not synonymous with digital layouts. Computer scrapbooking simply means you've added a little technology to your toolbox. Many scrapbookers enter this arena slowly, experimenting with computer-printed journaling. Along the way they learn to use their computers to manipulate images and perhaps...to create their own papers and embellishments!

Create a Monogram

If you love the look of oversized monogram letters, you'll love the fact that they are easy to create. Simply type a letter (400-600 point size) in the desired font and reverse print on the back of patterned paper. Cut out with a craft knife and add to your page.

Trudy Sigurdson

EASY ACCENT

An attractive digital font and a computer printer is all that is necessary to create a bold embellishment.

This reverse-printed letter is only a few steps away from becoming a beautiful, custom monogram. Carefully trim it and apply it to a background.

Q + a

Digital scrapbooking seems expensive. What do I need to get started?

A computer and a printer will significantly increase the creativity of any scrapbooker. Also consider investing in a few more tools. A digital camera will allow you to easily transfer images to your computer, which you'll be able to edit, print and even upload the photos to the Internet. A scanner will enable you to create digital images of photos, negatives, and more. Finally, invest in image-editing software so you can bend the boundaries of your creativity when working digitally.

Isaac loves his morning hair and discovering this song has made him more committed to it than ever. There was a recent day when he was so adamant about going to school with "party hair," that I decided this was one of those battles I really didn't need to win.
Left: Apr 05   Below: Mar 04

What's everybody looking at?

It's your hair. It had a party. . .

Well why didn't you say so?

Debbie Hodge

Layer Fonts

Spice up titles and journaling blocks with a mix of complementary fonts. Font mixes work best with three to five different fonts. Keep readability in mind—funky fonts are best used for a few keywords of larger size.

DIGITAL TERMS TO KNOW

To the uninitiated, discussions and instructions dealing with digital technology seem to take place in a foreign language. Learn a few simple words, however, and you can be speaking with the natives before you know it.

clip art: digital art file that can be downloaded from the Internet or from a disk that can be used as is on a digital scrapbook page or printed on paper

download (to): to transfer a file from the Internet to a computer

filters: artistic effects found in image-editing software that can be applied to images

font: digital type face—thousands of styles are available for download or on disk

image-editing software: software that allows you to digitally edit, alter and crop images

image manipulation: the act of digitally editing, altering or cropping an image

reverse print: to print in reverse, aka "mirror-image" printing

spot color: to add color to a section of a black-and-white image

text wrap: to situate computer-generated text so that it hugs or wraps around the edges of an image

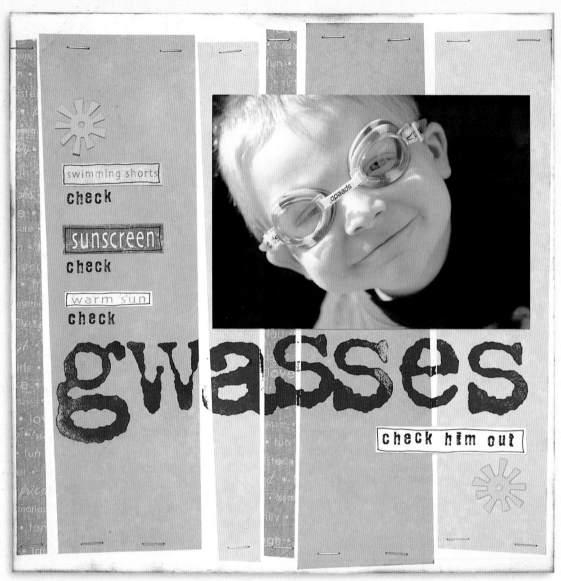

swimming shorts
check

sunscreen
check

warm sun
check

gwasses

check him out

Susan Cyrus

Add Spot Color

This traditional paper scrapbook page gets its digital punch from a little image manipulation. To create spot color such as this, start with a color photo. Copy the photo and convert the copy to black-and-white. Layer the black-and-white copy over the color photo. Use the eraser tool on the portion of the black-and-white photo in which you'd like color to show through.

THE BENEFITS OF DIGITAL SCRAPBOOKING

Most learning curves have some sort of ouch-factor involved. It often feels safest and easiest to stick with what we know. However, if you persevere, you'll find that mastering some digital skills offers scrapbookers an incredible payoff. Listed here are just a few of the benefits.

Total creative control Digital scrapbookers have complete creative control over things such as color and texture.

Save money on scrapbooking supplies Use digital backgrounds and accents over and over again. Mistakes can also be deleted without the fear of wasted supplies.

Easy to share Digital scrapbook pages can be e-mailed to friends and family, or burned to CD and given as a gift.

Ready for the Web Finished digital pages can be easily converted to Web-friendly files for Web sites or other digital presentations.

Use a Digital Kit

Creating digital scrapbook pages is easier than you might think if you use a digital page kit. Digital page kits include everything needed to create digital scrapbook pages. This kit includes a font, digital papers and digital accents. The artist simply downloaded it and dragged and dropped the papers and accents onto her digital palette.

Amber Clark

Ann Hetzel-Gunkel

Go Completely Digital

At first glance, this page looks as if it is made from paper, ribbon and traditional scrapbooking accents. But it is completely digital. Digital scrapbook pages often look indiscernible from their paper counterparts.

Beautiful Baby Pages

Create layouts worth cooing over

Where Did You Come From, Baby Dear?

Where did you come from, baby dear?
Out of the everywhere into the here.

Where did you get your eyes so blue?
Out of the sky as I came through.

What makes the light in them sparkle and spin?
Some of the starry spikes left in.

Where did you get that little tear?
I found it waiting when I got here.

What makes your forehead so smooth and high?
A soft hand stroked it as I went by.

How did they all just come to be you?
God thought about me, and so I grew.

But how did you come to us, you dear?
God thought about you, so I am here.

George MacDonald

January 2005

caroline

Judith VanValkinburgh-Garber

Babies are always more trouble than you thought—and more wonderful.

Charles Osgood

Create Perfect Infant Pages

Scrapbook your baby photos on pages as unique as your child

Many scrapbookers begin keeping albums after the birth of their first child. They want to showcase the miracle of their baby and document the infant's growth. As their family increases in size, they begin albums for each new child. While scrapbook pages celebrating their children's later years may actually be more accomplished, these early scrapbook pages are always special because they blossom with the excitement of holding a new life.

Kathleen Broadhurst

Sweet One

As soft and sweet as a baby's skin, this page sighs "infant." Gentle pink printed papers form the foundation for the double-matted photo. Delicate ribbons, a necklace of acrylic flowers and a spray of pink flowers, jewels and a swirled heart are among the beautiful embellishments on the layout.

Ribbons seem to be the embellishment of choice for scrapbook pages—especially baby pages. Any ideas for more unique embellishments?

Why not use bits of lace off of your baby's sock? Other ideas include smocked pockets, buttons, diaper pins, rattle handles, bib designs, hair bows and tiny earrings.

8 Days of You

A string of descriptive words supplies all the journaling this lovely page requires. Patterned papers, stamping and ribbons support the gentle photo. A tiny clock embellishment reinforces the "day-by-day" theme.

Ashley Calder

TAKING BABY FOR A FORMAL PORTRAIT

It is a rite of passage—that first formal portrait of your child. With some forethought, the experience can be positive from beginning to end and result in a superb professional photo.

Plan your timing carefully. If your baby appears to be coming down with the sniffles or is cutting a tooth, reschedule your appointment.

Plan the session. Early in the morning or shortly after your baby's afternoon nap—times when she will be her most rested and jolly.

Feed your baby before dressing her. Take extra water in a bottle or sip cup.

Dress your baby in comfortable clothes. Leave off the hat! (Babies who are not used to wearing hats find them irritating.) Pack two additional outfits for a quick change of clothing.

Take along your baby's lovey. Don't forget her special blanket or stuffed animal. Pack a small bag of other favorite toys.

Plan to arrive at the studio 10 minutes early. This helps your baby get comfortable with the environment.

Allow the photographer to direct the photo shoot. It is her job to know how to interact with your child. Let her do her job. Help out only if requested.

Your child may fuss. That's normal. But if fussing turns into extended wails, cancel and try the shoot another day. Even if the photographer can coax a smile out of your baby some time later, those post-cryathon photos won't be the most flattering.

Break the Rules Beautifully

Think outside of the box (or playpen)

You want your baby's photos to be as perfect as the child, but that doesn't mean that all your pictures need to be formal. In fact, scrapbooking snapshots, those spontaneous photos of your baby involved in her day-to-day activities, results in pages that capture the true essence of your child. So set aside your preconceived "rules"—ideas of what a baby scrapbook page "should" look like—and lean into your own creativity.

Rule #1
Photograph the WHOLE Baby

Sometimes a few select pieces add up to more than just a whole...they add up to a whole lot of love. Take photos of your baby from all angles. Crop the pictures and use them together on a spectacular page.

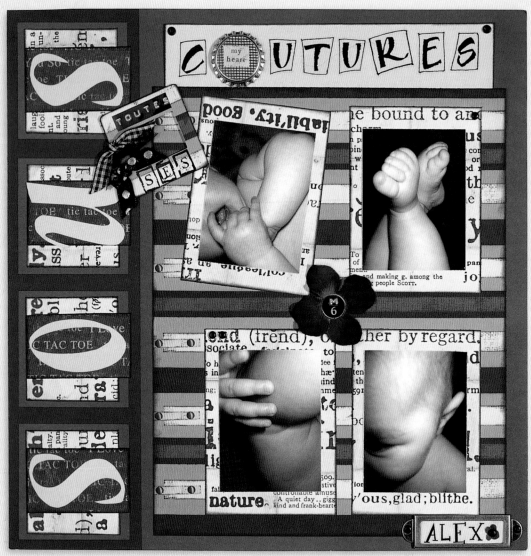

Julie Gauthier

Rule #2

Wait to Take the Photo Until...

A baby can convey emotion in many different ways. If you happen to take a photo of your child with his eyes closed and you love it, use it!

> *After a long Ohio winter full of coats, hats, and bundling, this was one of our first warm and sunny days. I just loved seeing Shelby light up and enjoy a small taste of spring,*
>
> Tracy Kuethe

Tracy Kuethe

Rule #3

Make Baby Beam at the Camera

The human connection when eyes meet and lock is an amazing thing. Photographs that capture that meeting of souls can be exceedingly strong. Scrapbooking these photos results in outstanding pages.

Kelli Dickinson

Turn Baby Toward the Camera

Rule #4

Capturing a baby in the middle of exploration is a perfect road to perfect photos. Restrain yourself from calling out his name, clapping your hands and otherwise interrupting his focus by trying to get him to turn toward the camera. (A baby's backside is so adorable, why not photograph it?!)

old pianos, as she did when she was a little girl. 1 January 05

Tapping a tune on Grandma's

child's Play

It holds an appeal that grabs you every time you walk past. You are drawn to it and reach up to hit a few keys. I'm not sure what it is, maybe its just that it makes noise, and a different sound every time, or maybe it is that you are in control of the sound?

Rachel Axton

" This piano is seeing its third generation of children, and even though it is old and out of tune (and much of the time neglected), it still has the same appeal to this new generation as it did to me when I was growing up, and my mom when she was growing up. I love that this photo captures my child's pure innocent curiosity. **"**

Rachel Axton

Rule #5
Make Sure You Can See Baby's Face Clearly

A child's view of the world is a magical thing, and those who recognize it can share in the wonder. Taking photos of the world as a child sees it results in strange and utterly unique pages.

We don't see things as *they* are,

we see them as WE are.
—Anais Nin

Ella, March 2005
Almost 3 months

Janet Ohlson

Mav - 5 mos. old

THE THINGS WE PUT UP WITH FOR fAShiOn

Lindsay Moore

Rule #6
Tidy Up Baby's Appearance Before Taking the Photo

What could be cuter than a baby whose ribbon or hat has slipped? Or an infant with peaches on his chin? Or a tot with one shoe off and one shoe on? Not much! So save yourself the effort of tidying up your tyke and just take the picture. You'll love the way it turns out.

Only Scrapbook Baby at Her Charming Best

Your baby serves up more than just gummy grins. She pouts, she crows, she cries, she bellows. Photograph her many sides and expressions and scrapbook them. You'll find yourself laughing over the intricacies of your tiny person in years to come.

Such a **face**! We had been trying for months to get your pouty lips on film. Success with Katie's help. I squealed as the image came up on the camera. You do this face everytime you are unhappy. Which, as you approach 2... is more frequent. We love to make the same face back to you until you laugh with delight! It's hard to say no to that _face_. Who can resist a good **pout**?!

100% genuine

2004

Felicia Krelwitz

I want to include my handwriting on my scrapbook pages, but I cannot write in a straight line. Help!

There are several tricks and tools to help you keep your handwriting tidy. Invisible ink pens can be used with a ruler to create straight line guides for handwriting. The ink then disappears as it dries. Journaling templates are available to also aid this endeavor. Or, simply use ledger patterned paper.

Rule #8

Only Dress Baby in Her Sunday Best

Forget the Sunday Best outfit and dress Baby in her birthday suit instead. Those dressed-down photos that show every inch of her perfect body will make you want to nibble the print and press kiss marks all over the finished scrapbook page.

Rolanda Heston

Rule #9

Take that Pacifier Out of Baby's Mouth!

Whether or not you're an advocate of pacifiers, you'll love those photos of Baby at his most relaxed. Photograph your child in his favorite environment, wrapped up in his own special world of imagination.

Anabelle O'Malley

" *...We were getting ready to paint his room, so all of the books had been taken off the shelf and placed on the couch in our guest room. I got sidetracked with something. A few minutes later I walked into the room to find him sitting amongst the books and reading quietly on his own. Of course I grabbed my camera and began snapping away. ... I hope he is always as enthusiastic about reading as he is now!*

Anabelle O'Malley "

Wonder at the Miracle of Your Baby

Celebrate your infant with remarkable page ideas

Delicate. Shell pink. Your baby's ear was designed to capture your whispered "I love yous" and magically convey the emotions to her heart. The idea of such a miracle raises a feeling of wonder within a parent. Once "The Rules" have been put to sleep, it becomes easier to focus on creating scrapbook pages that convey that Wonder! (The poems on the following pages are our baby gift to you. We hope you'll find a use for them within your scrapbooks.)

Shelly Umbanhowar

Wonder at Your Sleeping Baby

Hush little child and close your eyes,

Travel to Dream Land through starry skies,

Visit some ponies with manes of gold,

Sail on a ship with a jewel-filled hold.

Fly on a carpet or whirl through the air,

To find a sweet mermaid with miles of hair.

She'll gift you with smiles and a dream-filled comb,

To be placed in your scrapbook when you return home.

Princess

Inked pieces of pale pink patterned papers are layered to create a background for this sleeping beauty. Fluffy ribbons embellish the page, while template letters provide a vehicle for a minimal journaled sentiment. A rub-on word applied to one of the photos completes the sweet layout.

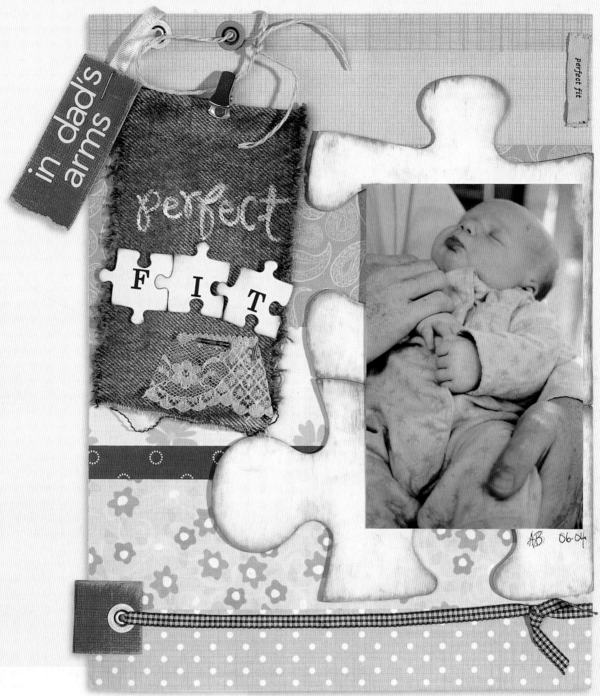

Ashley Calder

Wonder That Humans Can Be so Small

My hands are used for many things
For work, for sports and chores,
They push a mower cross the lawn
And pay bills when the day is done.
But when you need to rest in them
My hands are always yours.

Perfect Fit

The fatherly hands cradling his child show that this duo was destined to be together. Painted oversized puzzle pieces serve as a photo mat, and a piece of denim, clipped from the mother's shirt, acts as a foundation for the creative title.

Kiss Me, I'm Irish

Kiss this little guy, if you dare. (Although he doesn't look as though he's inviting affection. In fact, he looks like he'd rather play than pose!) Nevertheless, his darling photo is snapped and mounted on a background of green patterned papers. Ribbon-strung journaled tags tie up the layout.

ALL WIGHT, GWAMAW! ONE MORE PHOTO BUT NO MORE KISSES! Poor Camden, he gets so tired of Grandma and her Camera! His expression says it all in this photo. 2 years old

Sue Fields

KEEPING A BABY JOURNAL

The months of pregnancy are filled with "must-dos." There are appointments to keep, a nursery to decorate, shopping for a layette, announcements to send and much more! No matter how you may wish to keep up with your scrapbook, it may be impossible! So keep a detailed journal to help you remember all those important thoughts and events you will eventually want to include in your album.

- How you knew you were pregnant
- How you found your OB/GYN or midwife
- The highs and lows of your pregnancy
- When you first felt your baby move and how you felt at that moment
- How you told your family you were pregnant
- Whether or not you chose to know the gender of your baby and why

- How you decided on your nursery design and who helped you decorate
- What the process of selecting a name was like— what were the contenders
- How much weight you gained (and how quickly you lost it after the birth)
- What birthing classes were like—what you wanted to learn and what you did learn
- What pregnancy books did you read
- How you selected the birthing facility you settled upon
- Who was at the birth and how they responded to being there
- What the birth was like—how long labor lasted
- What you thought the moment you first laid eyes on your baby

Laughter

You are typically a very happy little boy, but when you find a funny, you take full advantage of it. Complete little belly laughs. Giggle fits like no other. Your laughter is contagious. Your spirit is irresistible. You make me smile. I love you my silly little boy!

Kelli Barringer

Kelli Barringer

Wonder at the Way Your Baby's Smile Lights up the Room

A baby laughs and deep inside,
A tiny smile begins to grow,
It buds and blooms and blossoms 'til
The joy has nowhere else to go.
At times like this it's often best,
For moms to join the giggle-fest.

Laughter

Belly laughs. That's what this photo is all about. And if the expression on the baby's face doesn't convey the message clearly enough, the journaling on a large office tag fills in the blanks.

Fountain Fun

Experts say that it is through play that toddlers learn. Water play may provide youngsters with their first lessons in physics but, let's face it, it's just plain fun. Layered blocks of patterned papers full of star bursts, stripes, and polka dots convey that frolicking feeling exuberantly.

Wonder at Your Baby's Fascination at the Wide, Wonderful World

Pat a cake, rattle shake,
Oootch, crawl, walk, run,
Ball throw, stop, go—
A baby's job is never done!

Another Sunday spent at Mama and Papa Stark's means food, fun, and lots of getting into mischief! Mama had just bought a fountain to go in the front yard. The two little hoodlums insisted on playing in the water. Splashing and giggling, you two had so much fun!

August 2004

A boy, mischievous to the Nth degree

FRIENDS

Nicole Stark

Nicole Stark

Come Out and Play

Every baby has a shining spirit, even if, sometimes, that spirit plays hide and seek. The exuberant patterns and colors on this layout complement this baby girl's toothy grin and bubbly personality.

Wonder at Your Baby's Zest for Life

Seaside shells of gentle pink
Whisper and sigh.
Pale yellow is a chicken's fluff—
Peaceful and shy.
Some colors shout and whirl and sing
And they are quite a different thing!

You are always so shy and quiet around people you don't know well, everyone finds it hard to believe what a little goofball you are at home. But suddenly, at a birthday party this past weekend, you were your silly little self right in front of everyone: jumping, laughing, talking. I'm so happy you finally decided to

come out and play.

And I hope this is just the beginning of everyone else finally getting to know the happy little girl that we've known all along.

Angi Stevens

+Qa

I love bright, bold patterns, but they can overwhelm a scrapbook page. How can I temper them?

When it comes to strong patterns, sometimes less is more. Try using these patterns sparingly in the form of a photo mat, a page border or a fun series of punched shapes. A vellum overlay also will tone down the pattern.

Boots

A colorized black-and-white photo beautifully calls visual attention to this little doll and her special pink boots. The pink and black patterned paper background supports the two photos. Journaling is distributed between the solid block and strips. A ribbon strung through decorative eyelets creates a border for the focal photo.

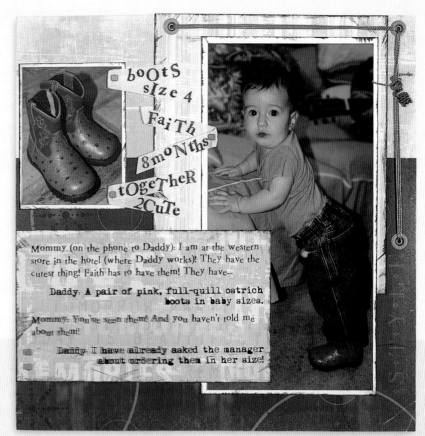

boOtS sIze 4 FaiTh 8moNths tOgeTheR 2CuTe

Mommy (on the phone to Daddy): I am at the western store in the hotel (where Daddy works)! They have the cutest thing! Faith has to have them! They have...

Daddy: A pair of pink, full-quill ostrich boots in baby sizes.

Mommy: You've seen them! And you haven't told me about them!

Daddy: I have already asked the manager about ordering them in her size!

Tamara Joyce-Wylie

Lynne Rigazio Mau

Blue Jean Baby

Denim is so versatile. Dress it down with a sporty hat, or dress it up with just the right purse, and you've got an outfit that can go anywhere. Patterned papers work well as a background for this page. An embellished file folder holds additional photos of the tiny model.

Wonder at Your Baby's Sense of Style

Fashion is my passion,
It is blatant that it's so.
And soon I'll own a credit card!
Just watch my wardrobe GROW!

Kathy Irion

Wonder at the Bonds That Form

Once you waited next to God
Wrapped in His holy light,
You stayed there rocked by angel wings
Until the time was right
To join our little family
And hear your chosen name.
(I've waited for you all my life
I'm happy that you came!)

A New Baby Is Like...

The arrival of a baby can teach a sibling so many
things: to share, to protect, to love without reserve.
The right photo can capture this bond, and a design
utilizing ripped patterned papers in the warm colors
of earth supports the theme. A beautifully journaled
tag, strung with ribbons and decorated with a clip,
and a few buttons and a clock hand are all that are
needed to complete the page.

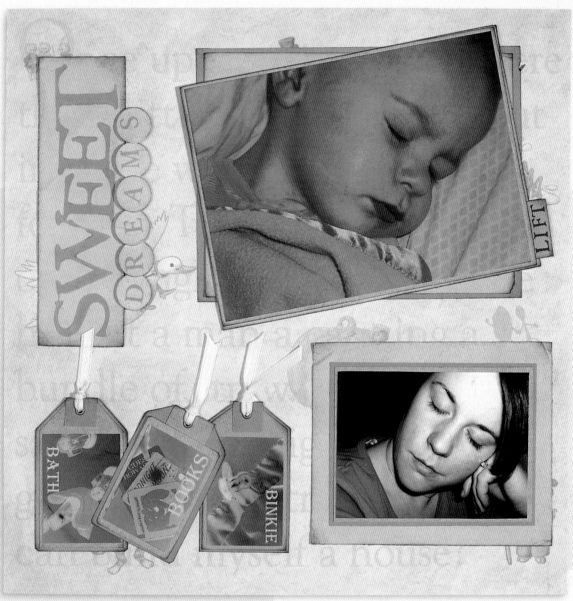

Pamela Turos

Sweet Dreams

A mother's saga about "sleep training" her baby is detailed behind the focal photo. While not pleasant for either baby or parents, the experience brought about important realizations.

Wonder That This Blessing Is Yours to Raise

I will wrap you up in blankets of love,
Woven by angels residing above.
Warm and safe you will be in my arms,
With Mommy and Daddy to shield you from harms.

Miniature Tag Books

Document 12 Months of Baby Milestones

Tag books are a great way to add information to a page. Although they are small enough to fit nicely as an element on a scrapbook page, they can hold extra journaling and photos. Create a special tag book that features the first 12 months of your baby's life.

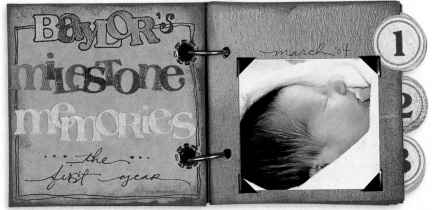

Tia Bennett, Photos: Amy Grendell

12 Months at a Glance

This tag book featuring baby Baylor's first year of life contains 24 pages—two pages for every month. The journaling details the infant's developmental accomplishments and is accompanied by an adorable photo.

Tia Bennett, Photos: Amy Grendell

Effortless Construction

Create a tiny tag book by trimming sheets of coordinating patterned paper into blocks. Adhere the two blocks together to create double-sided pages. Mount photos and journal. Add tabbed dividers of punched paper circles for easy reference. Decorate the booklet with paper strips and stickers.

Tia Bennett, Photos: Amy Grendell

Tia Bennett, Photos: Amy Grendell

Easy to Bind and Attach to Your Page

To bind the pages, simply stack finished pages in desired order. Punch a set of holes along the left side, insert jump rings and embellish with ribbon. To attach the book to your page, set two eyelets on the page background. String ribbon through the eyelets. Tie the ribbon to the book's binding rings. When adding tag books to pages, be sure your page background is sturdy enough to accommodate the added weight. Heavyweight cardstock, foam core and buffered cardboard can all be used to reinforce the background page.

Cooking Up Boy Pages

Whip up boy pages that are a special treat

Boys are complex—relaxed one moment and in full-throttle motion the next. They meet life head-on—resulting in assorted trips to the emergency room to be patched up. As soon as they are set loose, off they go again to find the nearest skateboard to leap on or chair to leap off. When not in conquer-the-world mode, boys can be exceedingly thoughtful and downright sweet. There is nothing like a hug from a son to melt a mother's heart, and if he is inspired to say, "I love you, Mom," her heart will puddle even without the hug.

Scrapbooking boys can be a challenge if for no other reason than the fact that it is difficult to shoot photos of a moving object. But if you are lucky enough to snap that picture at just the right moment, you'll hold in your hand a photo so strong that it demands its own layout. And if you have mastered the skill of walking on cat's feet, you may even be able to creep up and snap your son's picture when he is engrossed in some quiet-time activity.

The recipe for scrapbooking boy photos isn't always straightforward, but there are some guidelines that can help. Just remember to stay on your toes and go with your instincts. One set of rules never applies because boys are, quite simply, their own dish.

Shannon Taylor

 Snips and snails and puppy dog tails. That's what boys are made of!

Unknown

The Secret Recipe for Great Boy Pages

Follow these instructions to make scrapbook pages featuring your favorite little guy

Begin with an all American boy. You'll know a good one when you see one. They tend to grin from ear to ear. Their fingers are usually a bit dirty, as are the backs of their necks—signs of a child who really knows how to play. More often than not, they are wearing denim and tennis shoes. And while their cheeks are rosy and round, please don't squeeze.

Shannon Taylor

How can I prevent ribbon from bunching on my layout?

Try stitching the ribbon to the background or using a tacky, wet adhesive (allow ample time to dry). Or, use adhesive-backed ribbon.

So Lucky

This scrapbooker's desire for great photos has resulted in new experiences for her children. While on her father-in-law's farm, the artist contemplated her good fortune at being able to photograph her son in this location. Those thoughts led to the "lucky" theme of the page. The homespun background consists of strips of ribbon and rickrack.

Tricks

Even at 3 years old, this boy has skills. To properly showcase this thrill-seeker, the artist mixes a variety of playful patterned papers, which she first inked to give them a dirtied-up, boyish feel. The tile is created with chipboard blocks covered with patterned paper and embellished with rub-on letters.

Katie Rose

Nicole Schuiling

> **"** *You can call me Boy!* **"**
>
> Joshua, age 2,
> son of scrapbook artist
> Kelli Dickinson, responding
> to the question
> "What's your name?"

Sam

Boys never stop moving—just ask any exhausted parent! And so moms and dads who want to keep up with their little men look for quick and easy ways to scrapbook their photos. This terrific page proves that it can be done. Layered papers, cardstock stickers, rub-on letters, brads and a few fibers join three pink-cheeked photos to make up the page.

Choose Your Boy Carefully

All American boys come in a variety of shapes and sizes. You really can't tell what is inside simply by looking. And that old wives' tale about being able to tell how sweet it is by rapping on it with your knuckles is just plain nonsense! (We don't recommend trying.) Instead, take time to get to know your boy by photographing him with friends as well as alone.

> *I want a brother! But a dog would be cool too.*
>
> Ryan, age 6, son of scrapbooker Mandi Pierce, when asked whether he would rather have a baby brother or sister.

Cousins

This layout is especially important to the artist because her son has not been able to hang out with his cousins for three years. The right-side border is created with preprinted phrases set inside conchos. The colors are inspired by the boys' T-shirts.

Jennifer Gallacher

Let Your Light Shine

This layout features colors, patterns and textures appropriate for showcasing the playfulness of a young boy. But also used are soft ribbon accents, hearts and a pre-printed daisy to complement the innocent shine of his young face.

Nicole Jackson

I wanted to see if it was aerodynamic!

Luca, age 4, son of designer Andrea Zocchi, on why he threw a book across the living room.

Missy Neal

Welcome

This layout is all about the photo, which the artist enlarged, converted to black-and-white and printed on a wide-format printer. Chipboard letters in a mixture of colors, styles and sizes beckon the reader to come play with the subject.

Add a Spoonful of Sugar and Allow to Simmer

Once you have selected the perfect all American boy, add a dollop of sweetness. While sweetness can come in a variety of forms, the pink kind is rather special and often overlooked. Trust us when we say that not even a flurry of ribbons or a silk flower can make a true American boy look less than rough and tough. Once sweetened, set in a quiet place and allow to rise.

Cowboy Cameron

This page shows first and foremost what a character the model is, but it also is a testament to his mother's belief that the imagination is the greatest entertainer of all time. To create an appropriate background for this cowboy, all of the patterned papers were distressed. Achieve the pinwheel pattern by pulling the edges of the paper over the rounded edge of a dining room table. Sand on the curve. Finish by adding brads to resemble the studs of a saddle.

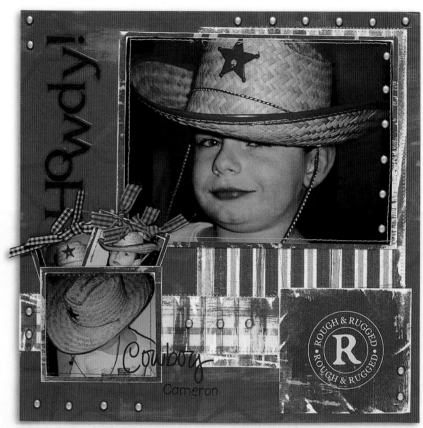

Deirdra LeBlanc

The S's of Sean

Silly, sneaky and utterly super, this little boy has captured his mother's heart. He's featured within a frame created with four thick strips of patterned paper that are mounted off-kilter. The large "S" that guides the eye across the page is hand-sketched. The rub-ons snaking along the letter add the finishing touch.

Pam Callaghan

But I don't want to grow up and move away! I want to marry you, because I love you, and you are my mommy. I want to live with you forever!

Joseph, age 5, son of scrapbooker Erin Harrington, reacting to the comment that he would one day grow up, move away from home and get married.

Wendy Inman

Create Art

Document a young child's creativity and use it as a catalyst for a creative evolution as he matures. The "art" booklet opens up to show examples of the model's masterpieces. To duplicate this idea, scan and reduce artwork. Print the reduced images onto white cardstock and insert them into a premade mini book that easily adheres to a layout with an adhesive of medium tackiness.

Tell me more creative ways to include my child's artwork in my scrapbooks.

If you scan, reduce and print the artwork, there are several ways to include it. Slip it into a mini book, create a series of small accents or frame each tiny masterpiece. Also, consider scanning and enlarging pieces to use as background paper or photo mats.

Put Things in Motion and Mix It Up

After the sweetener is added, it is time to stir things up a bit. This is easy to do. Just provide your boy with a bike, a skateboard, a light post, a ball, a bat or anything else that can be considered a toy. Take more photos than you think may actually be necessary. You may find that some are out of focus and others show a child just exiting your frame. Select paper and embellishments that add energy to your layout.

Personality

Scrapbook pages can provide a window into a subject's personality. Here, the artist wished to convey how absolutely unique her son is. The nontraditional landscape format of the page is a nice complement to the bird's-eye view of the photo. The title is divided into syllables and printed in a variety of descriptive fonts.

Shelly Umbanhowar

Pool Party

Your local swimming pool may not have waves, but you can create fun motion on your scrapbook page with brightly colored patterned papers cut into wavy shapes. This digital page is created to appear multi-dimensional . Photos, tags and embellishments are layered to frame the focal image of a young boy sharing a splashingly good time with Dad.

Mikki Livanos

Happy

Could this be a future fireman? An aerial acrobat in training? Perhaps just a monkey boy at play? The background of this page offers several stamped motifs. The artist colored directly onto the rubber of the stamps with markers to produce this multicolored, faded and imperfect design. The stitching accents are stamped as well.

Nancy Kliewer

I have a new digital camera, and all my "action shots" are blurry. Is there anything I can do to change this?

Yes, first check the ISO setting on the camera. For action such as sports, you want the highest ISO possible unless it is a very bright day. You can also use the "sports" mode if your camera has one. The "sports" mode is often represented by an icon of a running man.

Add Some Spice for Kick

Add a pinch of pepper or chop up some chilies to add bite to your work. This can be accomplished with hot color palettes that include hues such as lime green, orange and red. But a photo with attitude can carry off the job even when scrapbooked on earth-tone papers. Enlarge the image until it fills much of your page. Crop in tightly on your boy's face and allow his energy and attitude to overflow onto the layout.

Peggy Severins

Oh Boy

This layout documents the mischievous nature of a true-blue boy who got caught playing in Mom's scrap room, gleefully making a mess. The monogram letter is handmade. Print a letter in the desired font at 600-point size. Before printing, choose "mirror image" in the print settings and print on the back of patterned paper. Cut out the letter and embellish as desired.

Unbelievably Blue Eyes

This little guy is going to knock the ladies off their feet with those incredible peepers. To offset this stunning enlarged photo, a border of patterned paper meanders down the right side of the layout.

Because I am a cereal gorilla! That's why!

Joseph, age 5, son of Erin Harrington, on why he eats so much cereal.

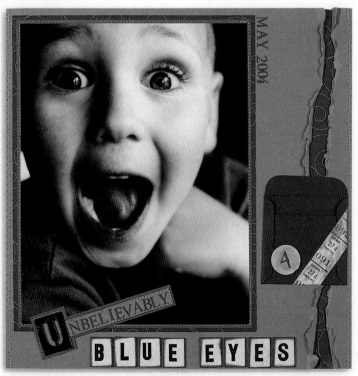

Cathy Goins

Amber Clark

Bad Boyz

These boys are bad to the bone, solid to the core. The artist printed her own transparency with descriptive words appropriate for these too cool dudes in shades. To duplicate the idea, highlight words with different fonts, type sizes and placement. Set the print settings to "transparency," and print onto a transparency, on the rough side to accept ink. Trim and fit to the page.

BAD BOYS WE LOVE

Sometimes boys are just bad, but sometimes boys are so "bad," they are good. Here is a brief list of "bad" boys we love and why.

Bikers – man and machine, rebelling against everything

Surfers – mop-topped, messy-haired, tanned and laid back

Rockers – loud, fun, artistic and wild

Activists – passionate, smart, in-your-face inspiring

In Uniform – respectful, authority figures, neat and a bit dangerous

Add Water and Chill

If things seem a little dull and dry, we recommend adding water. Boys simply can't resist rushing through a spray, or diving into a pool of icy wetness. You may wish to select a palette of cool blues and icy greens to convey a sense of cold for your brrrrr photos.

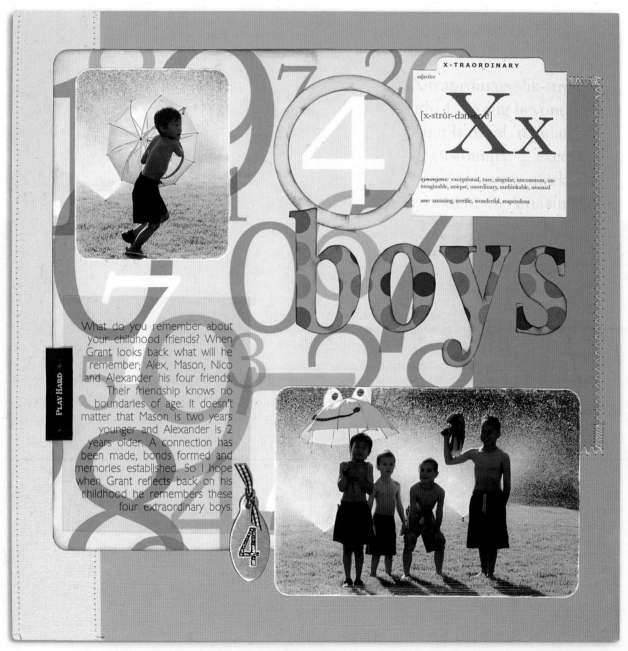

Summer Fullerton

4 Extraordinary Boys

Were it not for scrapbooking, the artist's son would not have tangible memories of his wonderful childhood friends. These photos were taken at the artist's son's sixth birthday party. With the sun shining behind the models and the sprinklers on, the photos are a great example of successful back-lighting. Three shades of complementary solid colors are used to create the background. A ring around the numeral, the simple monochromatic polka-dot pattern for the word "boys," and the themed index tab combine for a compelling title.

that face says...

...after playing for one whole hour in the water fountains at the Children's Museum. You were fully clothed and even wearing rain boots and a slicker, yet you managed to get entirely drenched down to your diaper! Luckily we brought a change of clothes because even with warm dry clothes, you were cold!

Marla Kress

Cold

Select a palette of cool blues and icy greens to convey a sense of cold. Use them with the right photo and you'll find yourself reaching for a blanket.

NEAT EMBELLISHMENTS FOR BOY PAGES

Get creative with your embellishments for boys pages! Take a look in your child's room or empty out his pockets for items you can include on your artwork:

- Tiny truck wheels
- Paper clips, rubber bands
- Rocks, sticks, shells
- Bottle caps, candy wrappers
- Old homework papers
- Broken shoelaces
- Pieces of assorted "stuff" he's taken apart
- Game cards, sports and trading cards
- Discarded CDs and damaged DVDs
- Comic books, children's magazines
- Old greeting cards, birthday invitations
- Tickets to sporting events and concerts

Allow to Age (Like Fine Wine)

Print favorite boy photos in black-and-white and scrapbook them on pages that have a heritage feel. Distressed papers that have been inked, sanded, folded and ripped automatically take on that antique feeling. Twill tape, rustic fiber, brads and other metal embellishments contribute to the aged and agelessly beautiful style. When done, you may wish to serve up a dish with a scoop of ice cream.

Amber Clark

Silence

This layered and distressed layout serves as a backdrop to a photo that caught a moment of sweet serenity. A mix of brown and black papers is embellished with a number of elements full of vintage charm.

C & O

Sanded patterned paper creates a rich heritage feel for this sepia photo. The edges of the photo are burned before being matted and mounted on chipboard. The edges of the photo mat and the handmade chipboard title letters are glazed, giving them a burnished appearance. Title letters are mounted on a strip of inked denim ribbon. A slashed pocket holds a journaling tag.

Mommy, who broke the moon?

Nathan, age 3, son of scrapbooker Nancy Boyle, upon seeing a crescent moon.

Charissa Stanton, Photos: Bernie Malin

Helle Greer

Little Boys Are Special

The ice-cream mustachioed, cherubic face of this model was all the inspiration this artist needed. The background is created with aged charm. Inside the mini file folder, which is sprayed with walnut ink, are two tiny journaling captions telling Stefan how special he is. Printed twill tape borders run along the top of the page while a strip cut from a printed transparency lines the right side.

 If you launched sunblock into the air it would cause the next Ice Age, huh, Mom?

Marco, age 6, son of photographer Joann Zocchi, displaying scientific gifts at a young age.

When Done, Simply Enjoy!

Your boy scrapbook pages will remind you of all the special times you shared with your son or special little guy. You'll be able to track his growth as he masters each challenge that appears in his path. And you will find yourself welling up with pride at the man he is becoming. Take credit for all you've done to contribute to his successful journey and enjoy!

Nancy Boyle

All my photos are starting to look the same. What can I do to make images that are more interesting?

Have fun, play with different angles, shadows, and reflections. Try placing your subject behind frosted glass such as a shower door. Experiment with different light sources such as a street light or a flash light. Get creative and think outside the viewfinder.

Looking Back 2005

The quote on this page should have resounding importance to any scrapbooker. "This page makes me stop to realize that my children are growing up so fast," Nancy says. "I need to worry less about a clean house and spend more time with my kids." This distressed page rests on a foundation of multi-width strips of coordinating patterned papers.

Marie Cox

Adversity

On the cusp of being a man, this boy has found a passion in sports. These photos illustrate the focus and determination he brings to his hobby. To give the page an aged feel, the artist converted the photos to sepia. She also used an edge distressor to help blend the photo edges with the patterned papers.

Middle Child

While starting a blended family, this artist created a special page for a special child—her stepson, the middle child of her husband's progeny. The journaling on this layout lists the characteristics common to middle children.

Anita Mundt

Is it OK to distress my photos with ink, paint and sandpaper?

Of course it is, as long as they are not one-of-a-kind photos. When cropping or distressing photos, it is best to use duplicate photos. That way, if something goes awry, you will still have the pristine originals.

Rough and Ready-Made Texture

Totally texturize for totally boy pages

Boys, they steal your heart with their rough and tumble ways. These mini men are bundles of perpetual motion and are best defined with words like "sturdy," "energetic" and "fearless." Create boy-themed scrapbook pages that capture and convey the essence of these adjectives with mighty masculine textures.

Colin has always been interested in motorcycles. The faster the better! This year, Colin saved up his money and bought this used KX80. Brett and Colin worked on the bike until they were able to take the bike to the track. Colin had a blast kickin' up some dirt!
August 2003

Chris Douglas

Tire Tracks

This page is smokin' hot with the look of burnt rubber. The thick-tread tire pattern is created by applying paint to a real bike tire. Roll the tire across cardstock. All kinds of textured items can be used in a similar fashion. Experiment with athletic cleats, sports balls, mesh or bubble wrap.

TEXTURE WITH BOYISH CHARM

There are lots of ways to add texture (or the illusion of texture) to your boy-themed scrapbook pages. Reach for unusual products and don't' be afraid to try new techniques.

- mesh—add it directly or use it as a mask when applying paint or stamping ink
- patterned papers in stripes, harlequin or distressed urban textures
- inky edges
- crumpled paper
- use a shoe to add a print
- caution tape
- sandpaper (black to look like skateboard)
- metal
- stencils and spray paint
- paint
- burlap
- cork

True Blue Denim

If you let them, most boys would happily live forever in blue jeans. This hardworking and sturdy fabric can be used ubiquitously on boy-themed pages. Create a page pocket by trimming a square of denim from an old pair of pants. Cut out the small pocket on the same pair of pants and sew it to the previously cut square. Stamp the title with acrylic paint and slip a tiny gift album into the pocket.

Chris Douglas

The Nitty and Gritty

The inky edges and torn-paper edges give this page a dirty feel. To re-create this look, rub a brown or black ink pad directly against the edges of the paper.

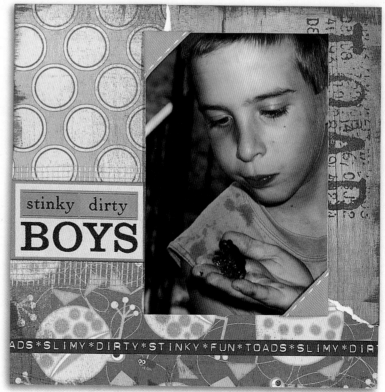

Chris Douglas

Sugar and Spice Girls
Fashion layouts for princesses and tomboys

"To look steadily at any one, especially if you are a lady and are speaking to a gentleman; to turn the head frequently on one side and the other during conversation; to balance yourself upon your chair; to bend forward; to strike your hands upon your knees; to hold one of your knees between your hands locked together; to cross your legs; to extend your feet on the andirons; to admire yourself with complacency in a glass; to adjust, in an affected manner, your cravat, hair, dress, or handkerchief; to remain without gloves; to fold carefully your shawl, instead of throwing it with graceful negligence upon a table; to shake with your feet the chair of your neighbor; to rub your face or your hands; wink your eyes; shrug up your shoulders; stamp with your feet, and so forth--all these bad habits, of which we cannot speak to people, are in the highest degree displeasing."

"The Lady's Guide to Perfect Gentility, in Manners, Dress, and Conversation"
by Emily Thornwell (New York: Derby and Jackson, 1856)

Thank goodness today's girls are unshackled and unashamed to show who they really are! We think they are utterly perfect and wouldn't change them for the world. (So let's tut-tut those Victorian rule-makers and celebrate what is right about our favorite little women!)

Patti Hozack

> *Etiquette is the barrier which society draws around itself*
> *as a protection against offenses the 'law' cannot touch…*
>
> "Hints on Etiquette and the Usages of Society," 1836

A Young Lady Is...

Learn to govern yourself, and remember that silence is often more valuable than speech

Today's young ladies know how to have a rocking good time. They enjoy being silly and rejoice in sharing their often off-beat sense of humor. They guffaw, snort, mug for the camera and roll around in all of life's giggles. And their good-natured antics are (lucky us!) contagious.

Valerie Yarbrough

+Q&a

How do I obtain a distressed look for my papers when I just don't have time to do anything elaborate?

Sanding paper is a quick way to achieve that distressed look. Just lightly scrub a piece of fine grit sandpaper over your paper. There are also papers made with a distressed appearance—no sanding or inking necessary.

Girls Just Wanna Have Fun

It is natural to bemoan the times we failed to capture in photos, but much more fun to crow about the ones we did photograph. One of those times is featured on this giddy layout featuring the artist's oldest daughter. The photo is featured on a page of funky patterned pastel papers. Inking adds dimension to the page. Ribbons and tags are tilted this way and that, as are title letters. The whole page screams, "fun!"

Muffin Muncher

Yum. Who can resist a truly spectacular muffin? Not this tyke! The photos are matted and mounted on papers that appear distressed. A rustic ribbon and shiny buckle border the bottom of the photos. The template "M" for muffin drives home the theme of this darling page. Photo turns and a cut-blocked title as well as brads complete the layout.

Raechelle Bellus

Through my journaling about the everyday minutia of family life, I have a greater understanding of my children's personalities, likes and moods. The photo on this page really speaks to me. It looks like my daughter is smiling, but she is really laughing. She tends to be a rather serious child so I love that my camera caught the happy gleam in her eye.

Lily Goldsmith

Girl

What a character! This great photo catches it and displays it with force on a scrapbook page that is a contrast between light-colored patterned papers and a dark background. A ribbon-strung buckle, embellishments and title blocks play up the model's great purple hat.

Lily Goldsmith

A Young Lady Should Caution Herself Not to Stare

Today's girls aren't afraid to look their neighbor directly in the eye. In doing so, they show that they are engaged and interested in the interaction. They survey their life choices in the same up-front manner and take life on as it comes at them. No diverting of eyes for these little women!

Kimberly Baltimore-Jones

Laney

This photo makes you simply want to play with the model's curls. The compelling photo is showcased on a background of gentle purple and green papers. Inking and distressing adds visual interest. Tiny tags, ribbons and poetic journaling complete the page.

Manners, Misses!

When calling, the following are considered gross breaches of etiquette:

- *To stare around the room*
- *To look at your watch*
- *To sit before being invited*
- *To overstay your welcome*

"Common Manners for Uncommon Ladies"

Be You

Scrapbook journaling provides a wonderful opportunity to share hopes and dreams for our daughters. This page includes a simple list that reminds the sweet model to be all she can be. This page is full of layers and textures. The mixture of papers works because the palette is consistently gentle, but the burlap, ribbons, brads, monogrammed letter, lace, buckle and alphabet dots add a heavy dose of texture and dimension, which give the layout strength.

Kelli Dickinson

Shine, Be Yourself

The layout certainly echoes the title of this page. Lots of micro beads just beg to be noticed. The title gleams. Flowers cut from patterned paper embellish the page, as do decorative ribbons.

Donna Bryant

+Q a

How do you create a micro-bead title without creating an utter mess?

Create the title inside the clean confines of a bead tray. Inside the tray, place title letters on which you have applied clear-drying wet adhesive (slightly tacky). Add the micro beads by shaking them over the wet adhesive. Allow 24 hours to dry. Lift the paper and gently shake off the extra micro beads before mounting the title on your page.

Tut Tut!

A Young Lady Never Becomes so Absorbed That She Removes Herself From Interaction

Even today's most social girls need downtime. This consists of private moments to wonder at the beauty of a flower, a cloud, a quivering bubble. They build dreamers who can imagine their way toward the building of better bridges, developing better medicines and making the world a richer place.

I Wish I Could Stop Time

The artist caught her daughter enjoying a quiet moment and snapped some photos. She then called her name and snapped the support image of her daughter laughing. The two equally lovely photos are scrapbooked on Victorian-patterned paper. Corners are clipped with a decorative corner punch, and the lace is inked for a vintage look. A flower, tiny tags and clock embellishment grace the artwork.

Theresa Lundström

All Girl

This little girl is caught up in her own private world, and we are privileged to watch her. Princess-pretty, surrounded by a palette of pink, the sepia photos that form the page border balance the focal and support photos in the center of the layout. A simple title, floral and ribbon embellishments and brads add to the mood of the page.

Kathleen Summers

Charlie & Fran

How often do you see a photo of a bubble about to burst on a child's nose or a stream of bubbles happily leaving a wand? These photos capture both events and are scrapbooked on equally creative layouts. Backgrounds of cut and inked patterned papers, brads, miniature embellishments, stencil letters and tape labels keep the mood reserved and yet never boring.

Wendy Gibson

Ladies Observe Fashion Dictates That Show Good Taste

Today's girls know that their fashion choices are one of the most obvious ways for them to define and express themselves. Through their choices, they let others know who they are as well. From that crazy hat to the vintage Halloween costume and pretty pink glasses, what they wear is definitely a part of who they are.

Michelle Klein

My Flower Child

Pictured is the artist's daughter dressed for her third Halloween party in as many days. At the last minute, the model decided that she wanted a new costume and this one was constructed on the fly. The photos are scrapbooked on a background of distressed and layered patterned papers. Ribbon cinches the center of the page and a bouquet of silk flowers supports the flower-child page theme.

Manners, Misses!

The first great fundamental rule of good taste is to be natural; and it is from an infringement of this that many of our worst mistakes proceed. In manner or style, affectation is the source of the most flagrant offenses against taste.

"The Lady's Guide to Perfect Gentility"

Girly Girl

Some photos just call out, "scrap me!" and this is one of them. Distressed pink patterned paper and supporting accents, including a pink slide mount, preprinted fabric tag and both gingham and polka-dot ribbon, are successfully used on the layout. A subtle stitched border surrounds the photo.

Kathleen Broadhurst

Curls and Fur

This fun and funky background captures the lovely shades of fall, and this little model is obviously ready for the nippy temperatures. The title is composed of letters within bookplates attached to the background with tiny brads. Small, cut pieces of decorative paper and a flurry of ribbons complete the page.

Tammy Brooks

66

Before I started scrapbooking, we only took pictures of big occasions. Scrapping makes me take pictures of ordinary things that probably would be forgotten in years to come. Like how my daughter's curls come out from this hat and the comments she gets about them.
Tammy Brooks
99

A Young Lady Does Not Go Outdoors Without A Hat and Appropriate Attire

Modern girls love the freedom that shorts, sandals, T-shirts and sundresses offer. They also understand the importance of vitamin D and sunscreen. Summer and spring provide girls with the opportunity to shrug out of their heavy winter garb and flit.

Sara McMartin

Be U

Warm weather is made for T-shirts, playgrounds and happy grins. This young lady knows all of that. Her happy-time photo is scrapbooked on a collection of patterned papers. Stamped letters add dimension. Ribbons, a fiber-strung journaling tag offering clues about the model's personality and a vibrant orange flower embellishment complete the terrific page.

Laughter

Summer fun radiates from this page featuring photos of a young mermaid enjoying her pool play. Patterned papers that appear water-speckled are layered beneath the photos. Baby blue brads, rub-on title letters, clear round stickers and dainty tags strung on fiber support the free-for-all, fun-for-all theme.

Exquisite

This layout catches the look of wonder on a child's face when she is exposed to new things. On this day, the artist took her young niece to a park to see the swans. To give the photo texture, it is printed on cardstock. The title is printed onto a transparency and layered over the photo.

Shannon De Witt

Linda Garrity

Manners, Misses!

One cause of the alarming prevalence of consumption among females in this country may, we suspect, be traced to the general adoption of a style of dress which is totally unadapted to guard the body from the influence of cold...

"The Lady's Guide to Perfect Gentility"

Tut Tut!

Trousers Are Better Worn by the Gentlemen

There is a time and place for skirts, and there is definitely a time and place for pants—especially a good pair of rough and tough blue jeans. They are the garb of choice for today's young ladies who want no skirts tripping them up on their mad dashes to the school swings or tangled in their bike spokes as they pedal to exciting destinations.

Sidewalk Chalk

This page captures so much: a child's creativity, a mother's love and the quintessential childhood sidewalk master-pieces. To mimic the look of chalk doodles on a wooden porch, rustic brown paper is mixed with fun pastels. The tags and faux stamp accents are all preprinted products.

Ashley Calder

CROP ETIQUETTE

Manners evolve as society changes. Old standards fall away and new ones are embraced. Good manners ensure that others are treated with courtesy, kindness and respect. Courteous scrappers only bring their best manners to crops!

- Clearly label all of your tools before packing your crop bag.
- Pack a water bottle to keep at the crop table.
- Offer to bring snacks for the group.
- Arrive on time.
- Set up your work area and do your best not to expand into the work areas of others.
- Share any supplies you no longer wish to keep. Share your tools.
- Bring and share newly completed scrapbook pages.
- Be supportive of others' work. If you have nothing nice to say, say nothing.
- Participate in cleanup, and don't overstay your welcome.

Ride

When tennis shoe meets pedal, watch out! That glorious feeling of freedom on the seat of a trike just can't be beat, as seen in this compelling photo. Torn and layered patterned papers form the background and frame the page. A piece of corrugated cardboard makes a rough and ready photo mat. Journaling and title appear on the tag.

Ashley Calder

Ashley Calder

Wait

When will the family fun begin? And how long can a young girl be expected to wait patiently? Long enough to capture the moment in a terrific photo! The image is mounted with a pink photo corner on patterned paper. A pocket holds a journaled tag next to a large stamped title. All elements are mounted on a piece of distressed corrugated cardboard that plays up the tennis shoe/wooden deck/blue jean feeling of the location.

+Q a

Is there a trick to using corrugated cardboard on a scrapbook page?

No trick at all! Just peel the smooth layer of cardboard away from the under portion to expose the ridges. Ink or paint the ridges for more definition. Do not mount photos directly on the cardboard.

Ladies Should Exercise Modestly but Avoid Overexertion

Exercise involves exertion and sometimes even (shhhhhh) sweat. Today's girls know what it feels like to raise their heartbeats, stretch their arms in dance and race after ducks in a park. Blood flowing, cheeks pink, they become motion—and that's a very good thing.

Lisa Turley

Precious Treasure

A captivating black-and-white photo of a young equestrian is showcased on a page that looks rugged and yet feminine. Patterned papers are inked for added visual interest. Ribbons create page borders, and tidy bows decorate the photo mat. A stencil tag displays the page title. Journaling appears on a tag that is slipped behind the photo. Brads, a button and buckle complete the layout.

> *Just looking at the expression on your face makes me smile. You were so filled with anticipation and excitement about visiting Aunt Becky and riding her horse...Your face glowed with excitement.*
>
> Lisa Turley

Shannon Taylor

To Go on Toe or Not to Go...

Is ballet a sport or an art form? Perhaps it is both! Certainly the physicality of ballet makes it as much of a workout as any other activity. This young dancer can attest to that! After years of barre exercise and floor routines, she's faced with a difficult decision—is she ready for toe shoes? Photos of the ballerina in contemplation and on-point are scrapbooked on gentle patterned papers. Painted twill, stitching, small tabs and ribbon flourishes make up the page. The title strips are suspended from a ribbon-embellished purse handle!

Kay Rogers

Funny Girl

Giddy playground fun is captured on this frolicking page. A combination of sassy pink patterned papers support three photos of an active little girl. Ribbons coordinate with the paper palette. A substantial journaling block balances the lower left corner of the layout.

Manners, Misses!

Costly cashmeres, very rich furs, and diamonds, as well as many other brilliant ornaments, are to be forbidden a young lady; and those who act in defiance of these rational marks of propriety make us believe that they are possessed of an unrestrained love of luxury, and deprive themselves of the pleasure of receiving those ornaments from the hand of the man of their choice at some future day.

"The Lady's Guide to Perfect Gentility"

A Smile Should Never Be Far From a Lady's Lips

Today's girls are at liberty to show their many faces. Some days are good. Some days are more difficult. Some days they feel like laughing, and others are pout or pensive days. When the mood to smile just isn't upon them, today's girls are often just as appealing without Cheshire Cat grins.

Theresa Lundström

10 Things I Love About You

For most scrapbookers, journaling is the most challenging part of the hobby, but without it, a layout has no context. Here, the artist uses a very simple journaling technique that results in quite a statement—listing 10 reasons she loves her daughter. The reasons are printed onto white paper and cut into captions. The edges are inked and then the captions are woven into the design via a train of flowing fiber.

PAGE PUBLISHING HINTS

Many scrapbookers hope to someday see their favorite pages featured in a magazine or book. If this is one of your private dreams, keep the following in mind:

- Use only original journaling (including poems) on your pages, or works originally published prior to 1923.

- Be careful about trademarks!

- Tell publishers if you are simultaneously submitting the same layout.

- Unless otherwise agreed upon, publish layouts only once.

- Submit your layout promptly to your publisher—missing due dates can hold up an entire project.

- Make sure all paperwork is completely filled out and signed.

- Package your artwork to assure safe delivery.

- Communicate openly with your publisher. Enjoy the relationship you build with the publishing industry!

Shannon Taylor

Pout

Scrapbooking can be about the good, the bad and the ugly. Perhaps this child does not now appreciate having her adorable pout put to film, but when she ages, she may delight in seeing her colorful moods captured for posterity. The photo is layered on a background of patterned papers covered with a printed transparency. An embellished tag made of paper squares mounted on a decorative ribbon balances the photo and creates a border for the image.

Manners, Misses!

The Secret of Looking Young.

A darkened brow, a morose countenance, an unpleasant expression, what are these but a winter landscape? A serene face, a sweet expression, a kind and gentle look: these are like a day in spring, and the smile on the lips is a ray of sunshine. Discontented people, you may notice, always look ten years older than they are.

Victorian London - Publications - Etiquette and Advice Manuals - The Lady's Dressing Room, by Baroness Staff, trans. Lady Colin Campbell, 1893

Wearable Art

Look fun and fabulous with these scrapbooking fashions

Have you ever headed to the mall in search of the perfect accessory, only to come home empty-handed and frustrated? Save yourself the trip by using your scrapbooking supplies and tools to turn out beautiful wearable art.

Heidi Schueller

Flip-Flops to Flip Over

After seeing what a little ribbon and a few silk flowers will do to an ordinary pair of flip-flops, you'll never look at store-bought footwear again. For these feminine footies, wrap grosgrain ribbon around the plastic straps until the straps are covered. Use heavy-duty double-sided tape to secure. Attach the flowers to the straps with fiber (thread through a needle and "stitch" through), tying the ends in French knots. The velveteen bow is attached with clear glue and the charm with a jump ring.

A CHARMING HISTORY

More than simple adornment, the earliest known charms are thought to have been rough stones carried by early man to ward off enemies. As cultures evolved, the appearance and properties of charms shifted as well.

- In ancient Egypt charms were worn by nobility and the wealthy. They believed that both here, and in the after life, charms would assure them of proper recognition and treatment—as befitted their status.

- During the Roman Empire Christians and Jews wore charms as identification, allowing them access to secret or restricted buildings and meetings.

- In the Medieval times charms were believed to protect the wearer and bestow tremendous powers in battle. They were also worn to show family connections or political or religious affiliation.

Choker and Beret Set

Turn a small length of ribbon into a fashionable choker necklace. Thread a ribbon charm onto a length of ribbon. Add tiny silk flowers, secured with decorative brads. Finish with a Velcro closure. The matching berets are created by simply covering the top of the beret with ribbon accented with a silk flower and decorative brad.

Heidi Schueller

Charming Bracelet

A simple charm bracelet benefits from some frilly fun when pretty ribbon slinks in and out of its links. Thread ribbon through bracelet links and knot at the end.

- In the early 20th Century Queen Victoria made decorative charms popular as embellishments.

- Charms became exceedingly popular in American during WWII when soldiers would pick up trinkets during their travels and bring them home to wives and girlfriends. Jewelers began mass producing similar trinkets.

- By the 1950s charm bracelets had become popular among American teens. Poodle skirts and sweater sets were all the rage, but no outfit was complete without a jangle around the wrist.

- Charm bracelets were discovered once again in 2000 when designers introduced charm jewelry in a wide range of styles. Today, charms are worn by females of all ages.

Heidi Schueller

Captivating Pet Pages

Construct warm and fuzzy animal-themed layouts

Attention class! Please put away your patterned papers, rulers and stickers. It is time to take some notes. I, Jay Schubert, am your instructor. Credentials? Of course! According to Owner, I am astoundingly intelligent—capable of learning any number of tricks in less than an hour. I am loyal to a fault. I don't nip or steal People Food off the kitchen table (although I am open to bribes, should you wish to sneak me a piece of your cheese pizza). As such, I am sure you will benefit from my thoughts and observations.

For the most part, the information I will impart is self-explanatory. I've compiled research from both personal experience and members of fellow species including those that fly, swim, crawl and have issues with lodged balls of hair. With the understanding that some or you may be visual learners, I have included rather splendid visual aids in the form of scrapbook pages. The subject matter focuses on "How to Live a Better Life."

So please turn to the next page and focus your attention. There may be a pop quiz at the end of this chapter.

Dogs come when they are called; cats take a message and get back to you later.

Mary Bly

Liani Suwandi

Pets Can Teach Us New Tricks

A kind word, scratch behind the ear or shake can make another's day

We all live on the same planet. We share the same air, water and food. We depend upon each other for companionship and safety. We may be friend, or we may become friends if given just a pant of a chance. So live your life looking for ways to bring us closer.

Christine Traversa

Q+a

How do I get my dog to hold still and look at the camera?

Get your pooch's attention with something he is really interested in. Hold his favorite ball or toy next to your camera as you take the photograph. Better still, try a doggie treat and you will have his undivided attention.

Zak

This page helps one little girl and her mother remember how kind this dog is, for he lives far away from them. The photo is converted to black-and-white to better work with the adorable patterned paper. Along the bottom runs a border strip, created by running a thin piece of cardstock through a Dymo machine. The strip is inked to give it more dimension.

It's What's Inside That Matters

Beauty is only skin deep. That's what the old saying tells us. But too often, swayed by our "Botox and body beautiful" society, we forget. Focus on finding the unique beauty in each of us, and the world becomes decorated with treasures.

Laura McKinley

My Protector

The dog is often the family protector, and the one pictured here is no different. The fabulous photo of a dog doing his duty is matted on fabric, which adds interest and texture without subtracting from the image. The frayed fabric edges add the rustic appeal of a well-chewed stuffed toy.

> " (Kostya) is not an active pet. It's difficult to do a page on her activities. She is not like a cat or dog that plays catch or with toys. "
>
> Jeryn Carlisi

Kostya Tszu

Wanting to capture the uniqueness of her family pet, this artist struggled with the page concept. She triumphed with an enlarged photo of the majestic creature, which she highlighted with animal patterned paper. The title is made with painted chipboard letters. The leaf embellishment is created with acrylic paint and stamps. The stamped twill tape is frayed at the ends for a rustic effect before being attached to the background with brads.

Jeryn Carlisi

Life Doesn't Stand Still, So Embrace Every Minute

There is a big world out there just waiting to be explored and enjoyed. So turn off the television. Take a break from chores and do something just a little bit crazy. It will help you redefine your boundaries and open up realms of possibilities you never imagined.

Mary McAfoos

How do I find just the right embellishment for a unique page?

You will be utterly astounded by the wide variety of embellishments available today. Many name-brand manufacturers (such as Harley-Davidson) have licensed their logo and look to craft manufacturers specifically for the creation of craft products and embellishments.

Free Spirit

This dog loves posing for the camera, especially when dressed in such cool duds. Layered coordinating patterned papers capture the tough-guy mood. The page is neatly embellished with chains, brads and folded ribbons for a speedy layout.

Naps Aren't Just for Babies

There is something wonderful about snuggling up and closing your eyes in the middle of the afternoon. Perhaps it takes us back to those infant days when we were somehow supremely aware that Mother was in charge, and we were safe. Relive those content moments and give yourself a break by coppin' a snooze now and then.

Kitty Lazy Days

The photo and title work in conjunction on this cat nap. The tightly cropped sepia photo is the star of the layout, however the bold title balances the image. Ribbon stretched across the layout horizontally frames the photo and ties up a tag.

Christine Traversa

Julie McCauley

Dog Tired

Up, up and...wait a minute. Time for a short commercial break. This lovable dog believes in resting a bit before hoisting the rest of its body onto the couch. The appealing photo is mounted above three pieces of patterned papers. Brads, buckle-strung ribbon and tiny alphabet beads make the layout downright perfect.

I have learned the true meaning of unconditional love and loyalty from my pets. No matter how bad your day has been or what kind of mood you are in, they are always happy to see you and to show you how much they love you.

Julie McCauley

Whistle a Happy Tune

When you smile, others smile with you. And those smiles generate more smiles and more smiles and more...until that single first grin is responsible for making the world a much more joyful place. Be the person who begins the pattern. Spread the word to spread the smile.

Angela Daniels

Cosmo and the Peeps

Cosmo, a tame lovebird, perches with a few friendly chicks—Peeps marshmallow birds from Easter. The playful patterned papers contribute to the silliness of the layout. The title is printed in the desired font onto plain computer paper. Textured pink card-stock is punched into circles and adhered with removable adhesive over the printed title. The printed paper is again run through the printer. The punched (and now printed) circles are removed and mounted on the page.

Guido

This page was created in memory of a sweet feathered pet. The large letter "G" in the title is created by tracing a die-cut letter onto green paper and cutting it out. The edges are inked using a makeup sponge and the lyrics "I will remember you" added. The words "time flies" on the clock, the journaling blocks and journaled words surrounding the photo infuse the page with emotion. Ribbons, a tiny frame and flowers contribute to the loving tribute to Guido.

Tia Bennett, Photos: Bay Loftis

There's No Place Like Home

It doesn't matter whether you live in a mansion or a cottage, an apartment or even a cardboard box. If you fill your abode with friends, food, song and laughter you will be "home." Home is where you are safe. Home is where you are loved. There truly is no place as special.

Raechelle Bellus

Box Buddies

These two cuties share a love for playing in boxes. The box theme is played up with a layered photo frame made of blocks of paper, which also sits on a background created from layered blocks of paper. The frilly pink papers and ribbons coordinate with the young model's pjs.

How can I find papers that match the outfits of those in the photos?

There are so many papers available today that matching papers to elements in photos isn't difficult. But if you want an exact match for your desired effect, simply scan the material you wish to match. Print the scanned image onto photo-safe paper and scrapbook!

Alex, the cat, died several years ago, and this photo reminds me that he was so loving and my daughter and him were inseparable. It's like he was a sibling.

Raechelle Bellus

We Benefit as Much from Play as Work

"All work and no play makes Johnny a dull boy" goes the old adage. It is a balance between work and play that affords us the most pleasure and progress. So take time out of your busy day to get in touch with the child inside, break loose and be silly.

Isabelle L'Italien

Capucine

To complement the cat's tabby coat, the artist selected patterned papers in warm reds and oranges that are just a bit more saturated than the orange fur. Torn notches are sponged with dark brown ink. Red ribbon, similar to the string the cat plays with, embellishes the page. Extensive journaling and brads complete the layout.

From (my cat), I've learned that even with humans, the best way to befriend someone or to create a relationship is to let them come to you on their own.
Isabelle L'Italien

Our Dogs

A fought-over toy broke, freeing two tennis balls but only one was coveted by both pups. One happily chews while his friend watches on with envy. For the title, paint is daubed onto stencil letters into the squares of a piece of patchwork fabric. The photo is matted onto a piece of distressed corrugated cardboard and embellished with a flower, plaque and button.

Pet pages are my favorite to create. There is no pressure to please the subject!
Christina Buckley

Christina Buckley

Age Doesn't Matter When Souls Touch

A friend can be any shape or color. Friends can also be any age. Friends who are older share their life-learned lessons and wisdom. Friends who are younger remind us of the benefits of being carefree and help us view the world less cynically. There is a place in our lives for both teaching and learning…a place for friends from many different generations.

Companions Always

Love comes in a variety of forms. This little pup obviously adores his elder. Photos are scrapbooked on a textured background of patterned papers and ribbon. Tags displaying additional photos are slipped into a decorative pocket.

Lisa Pace

PET PHOTO TIPS

They squirm and wiggle and never want to look at the camera! That's why photographing pets can be so difficult. Here are some tips that may make snapping pet photos a bit easier to accomplish.

- Get down on the same level as your pet.

- Focus on your pet's eyes. That's where personality and emotion are centered.

- Shake a toy to catch and hold your pet's attention or give your pet a toy to play with. (You may need a photo assistant to help.)

- Use fast film, ISO 400 or 800.

- Photograph your pet against a contrasting background.

- Shoot (I mean, PHOTOGRAPH) your pet in its natural habitat.

- Avoid using flash when shooting a water-housed pet.

- Anticipate your pet's action and movement.

- Take more photos than you believe you will need on your scrapbook page.

It Is Only Through Curiosity That Knowledge Takes Seed

Why is the sky blue? Why does the wind blow? Why do yellow and blue make green? There are so many questions out there just waiting to be asked. Don't be shy! Nobody will diss you for your curiosity. Just ask! With each question you'll find the world a more fascinating place.

Our Goldfish

This goldfish's short stay with the artist's family showed that her son is responsible enough to care for a pet. The title "g" is traced from a die-cut monogram onto patterned paper. The close-up shot of the fish is actually a duplicate of the original photo, enlarged and tightly cropped. Ribbons and a tag join a journaling block to complete the page.

Sally Cranney

Which Is Which?

This 8 x 8" layout alerts readers to the physical differences between these two seemingly identical turtles. The photo is matted on rich orange patterned paper and mounted on blue cardstock. The clover stamped title treatment is layered with rub-on letters. Stitching, ribbon and brads add dimension.

Stephanie Brown

You Don't Have to Be the Centerpiece at Every Party

Charm isn't about telling the best jokes in the room. It is about laughing sincerely at another person's joke. Courage isn't about stepping in front of an oncoming car. It is about stepping off the curb to pull another to safety. Knowing when to stand up and when to sit down, when to speak up and when to be silent, when to take chances and when to be conservative are important lessons that we must learn to be successful in life.

Yolanda Williams

My Dog Scooter

These eyes just beg for loving. The crop on the panoramic photo keeps your attention focused on those peepers. The matted stencil letters that create the title are secured with brads to a section of the photo. The torn-paper frame that encapsulates the original poem is created by tearing a section from a piece of patterned paper. The edges of the frame are secured with twine and brads.

How do I neatly curl the edges of paper once I tear it?

Use a small round object such as a pencil, pen or screwdriver. Gently roll back the edges of the paper and press them around the object until the paper retains the curl.

Spread Love, Spread the Word

The wise teach the seeking and the seeking open our eyes to new questions. Those that speak in barks and mews and human voices hear and respond to each other's needs. We celebrate life under the same sun and moon. We are bound to each other. This union is a starting place, and abiding love is where it takes us.

Martha Crowther

Dogs Rule

What a powder puff of a pup! It is hard to equate the word "trouble" with this ragamuffin. And if that's what he brings into the artist's life, he brings even more joy. A focal photo and supporting shots show how bonded these family members are. An extensive journaling block with highlighted words, a bone embellishment, mini charm-decorated collar and more make this page something to howl about.

Mine

This layout focuses on the relationship between kitten and child. Its clean, unembellished design shows that your layouts need not be complicated. The large photo is mounted on several pieces of layered patterned papers. A few brown, black and printed ribbons running vertically behind a classic black mat, two themed accents and a chipboard title are all that are necessary to support the engaging photo and heartfelt journaling.

The young girl trudges home through the snow with a smile on her face. She opens the door and climbs up the stairs. As soon as she reaches the top, the kitten races down the hall and jumps into her arms. As she buries her face in her kitten's fur, both smiles say the same thing--Mamma's Home!

Dora Phillips

Purr-affection

This page is a testament to the lesson in control and gentleness the artist's son learned from animals and also the sweet personality of the pictured cat. A bold title built around a sassy pun sits on top of the photo. A journaling block, embellished with a tiny collar and kitty images, creates a border across the lower edge of the page.

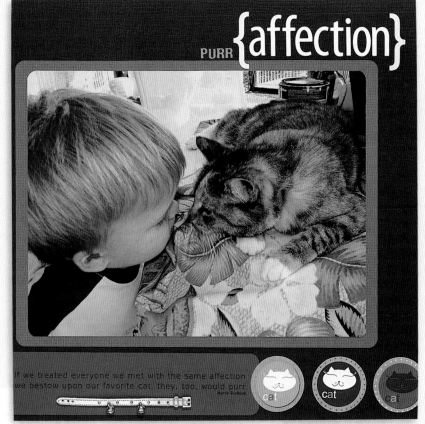

Linda Harrison

What if I just can't find an embellishment (or don't wish to invest in those that I find) for my layout?

Don't sweat it. Just use your circle punch to punch around portions of patterned paper (the kitty faces on this layout). Mat the images on larger punched circles and mount them on your page.

Best in Show

And now...ladies and gentlemen...the awards!

Before we hand out our trophies, we'd like to thank everyone who entered this show. There were literally hundreds of fantastic entries to consider, and the judges have found it very difficult to determine the winners. There were no predetermined categories and absolutely no judging standard and so we can't even begin to explain our rationale. All we know is that we loved these pages so much we wanted to adopt them. So hold on to your hats...here we go!

Yolanda Williams

Best Layout and Design on a Dog-Eats-Frisbee Page

Chest out, trot perfected, ears flying in the wind—that's a picture-perfect Scooter proudly clenching his Frisbee. This layout features a symmetrical design with a twist—the design could be sliced down the middle and each half would carry the same weight. But, unlike a traditional symmetrical design, each side is not a mirror image. Instead, the artist varied the elements by creating different blocks of information. On the left side is an enlarged photo of Scooter followed by a block containing half the title. On the right side, there is a block for journaling, support images and the other half of the title. The layout is unified by the paw-print accent. The curve of the title echoes the curve of Scooter's Frisbee. This page is one to howl over.

Best Use of Color and Black-and-White Photos
on a Turtle-with-a-Darling-Girl Layout

This page not only echoes a childhood refrain that elicits an eye roll from many mothers, it also displays the model's loving personality. The background is constructed with strips of patterned paper and cardstock. For contrast, a piece of mosaic-patterned paper is layered on top of the strips. To cut a clean, large curve out of the mosaic-patterned paper, a child's Sit 'N' Spin toy is used as a guide.

Patricia Milazzo

WHAT SHOULD YOU SCRAPBOOK ABOUT YOUR PET?

Taking photos of your pet at rest is a no-brainer. They simply look too cute all cuddled up on the couch they aren't supposed to be on, to resist. But there are other wonderful opportunities you may wish to scrapbook.

- The birth of your pet or your pet giving birth

- Your pet's first visit to the vet

- The first time your pet is carried into your home

- The store or home from which your pet was adopted

- The wild and wonderful array of food available for your pet and the one he prefers (and the reason).

- Your pet's most favorite and least favorite places to go

- The song that most reminds you of your pet and why

- Your pet's favorite person and their best shared activity

- Your pet's first birthday/anniversary with your family

- Your pet's idiosyncracies, behavior snafus and cute habits

Best Use of Corrugated Cardboard on a Cardboard-Loving-Kitty Page

Here we meet Max, who is a sucker for a good box. To show Max's adoration for all things cardboard and boxy, the artist created whimsical flower accents on corrugated cardboard. The positioning of the single kitty image conveys the sense that Max is peering from inside his little home.

Ashley Calder

+Q a

How do I make a corrugated cardboard element just like the one that won this FABULOUS award?

To re-create a similar accent, cut a block of cardboard and strip off the top coat of paper to reveal ribbing. Smear white paint on the ribbing and allow it to dry. Cover the cardboard with clear adhesive and press tissue paper into it while it is still wet. When dry, paint flowers on top. Outline the flowers with a black pen. Stamp the centers of the flowers and stamp a script motif across the entire block. Coat with clear gloss medium and allow to dry overnight.

Jennifer Gallacher

Best Photo of a Child Waiting for Turtle-Peeking

Pets not only complete a family, they offer wonderful learning opportunities for children. This little guy is learning patience as he waits for his turtle to come out to play. You can almost feel his held breath. The captivating photo is scrapbooked on textured blue cardstock. The large chipboard letters draw the viewer's eye directly into the image. Tiny ribbons add a touch of fun.

Best "Dog Collar" on a Little-Puppy-in-a-Little-Car Layout

This aptly titled layout expresses a sentiment pet owners the world over share: Pets are family. This pet became family on Christmas, when the artist gave him to her son. The photo of the new friends bonding is scrapbooked on textured blue cardstock. The orange ribbon attached to a D-ring resembles a collar. An inked journaling block completes the layout.

Alison Marquis

> *Pets love unconditionally. It doesn't matter to them who you are, what you look like, where you live, what you do or how much money you have. They will love you forever.*
>
> Cheryl Baase

Cheryl Baase

Best Use of Vellum and Stickers on an Uh-Oh Layout

Cats are drawn to fish like men are drawn to the television for the last tie-breaking inning of the World Series. Trying to pull the cat's head from the fish bowl is a bit like trying to separate your husband from the remote control. This great layout proves the point. The wonderful photo is featured on a background of patterned papers. Label tape journaling strips provide information. The stroke of genius is the fish bowl cut from water-patterned vellum. Fish stickers are layered beneath. The inked title is decorated with bits of orange, reminiscent of the tabby's fur.

Playful Pet Accents

Use polymer clay to create accents that are as playful as your pet

Fido and Kitty have their own beds, their own bowls, their own places in your heart. Why not give them their own page accents? Polymer clay is an easy and fun medium to work with when creating accents such as these. You can create embellishments that mimic the shine of an aluminum feeding bowl, or, if your furry friend will allow, you can set a paw- claw- or footprint in the clay for a piece of your pet that will last forever.

Fantastic Claytastic Creations

Polymer clay can be rolled, pushed and molded into just about any shape imaginable. Knead the clay to soften it and then freehand cut the shapes. After baking them (see polymer clay package for detailed instructions), coat them with clear gloss medium and detail them with permanent marker.

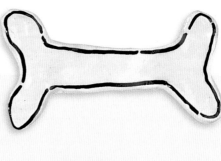

Shannon Taylor

MAKE A POLYMER CLAY PAW PRINT

Roll, mold and cut your way to easy accents.

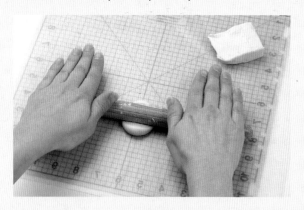

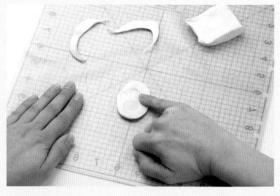

Roll a small piece of polymer clay in your hands until it is pliable. Use a dowel or rolling pin to roll the clay to ¼" thickness.

Cut the clay into a rough circle. Use your fingers to press paw imprints into the clay. Bake the imprinted clay tile according to manufacturer directions. Cool and chalk.

Can you believe she was born in our bed as we slept?

OLIVER KITTY

meow meow meow meow

The minute she was born

Oliver James named her after

him, but later called her Tiger.

We wish she still lived with us.

Shannon Taylor

Letters, Charms, and Paw Prints, Oh My!

This page is a purrrfect (Oh, come on! We couldn't resist!) example of the versatility of polymer clay. The title, paw print and cat accent are all created from the versatile medium. To create the title, push clay into a rubber mold and then put the mold in the freezer for about 15 seconds before removing the clay from the mold. The other two accents are created by rolling out small pieces of clay and stamping into them. Bake all of the clay pieces for 15 minutes at 275 degrees Fahrenheit and let them cool before painting and chalking them. Finish with a coat of clear gloss medium.

Festive Holiday Pages

Celebrate special times throughout the year

Sniff the gingerbread or latkes. Listen to the bells. Admire the flickering lights of the candles or the splashes of fireworks colors against the night sky. Holidays demand, with their smells, sounds and sights, that we set aside our work and our studies and enjoy! We step back and slow down, focusing on the people and the things that matter the most to us in the world.

Because holidays are so very important, we spend an enormous amount of time recording the special occasions with photos. Year after year after year after year, new photos are added to our holiday albums, and through these we can compare the growth and changes taking place in our lives. Babies in tiny butterfly costumes morph into super heroes before our eyes. Ornament collections started with a single perfect ball grow to weigh down sturdy boughs. Turkeys follow turkeys. New babies are born and outfitted in that well-loved butterfly costume.

Scrapbooking holiday photos is a way to continue the fun long after the last piece of mistletoe has been taken down. May the music of the holidays fill you with joy and may photos of your holidays fill your scrapbook albums with memories that bring back the tastes, stories and music of your holidays!

Hannah,

You're my Santa baby. Even when you're 50 years old, you'll still be my baby. Want to know a secret? I am Grandma & Grandpa Jenkins' baby. Yes, I'm the youngest of 3 children just like you. And hopefully you'll enjoy being the baby of the family. Parenting skills often relax and you learn from watching your sibling's actions.

You are so much like me when I was your age...mischievous, calculating and full of charm. I love that you'll always be my baby.

Mom

Susan Piepol

Blessed is the season which engages the whole world in a conspiracy of love...

Mabie Hamilton Wright

Great Holiday Pages
Begin with Great Photos

The holidays offer special opportunities and special challenges for photographers

The holidays are filled with wonderfully spontaneous moments that have scrapbookers grabbing for their cameras. Unfortunately, the circumstances surrounding holiday activities don't always offer easy-to-photograph moments. But with some forethought and a bit of know-how, you can snap away with confidence. And your photos will be as joyful as the holidays themselves.

Jennifer Turner

Q + a

How do I best capture fireworks on film?

To capture fireworks you first need a tripod as hand-holding the camera will cause blur. Use fast film, or a high ISO setting if you are using a digital camera, for the best results. And use a camera that allows you to keep the shutter open for more than several seconds.

America

Fancy Fourth of July fireworks are captured in photos and framed in slide mounts on this patriotic page. A young patriot displays his mini flag and a mini grin in the black-and-white photo. Twists and journaling embellish the flag patterned papers.

Magic

This photo of the artist's son definitely qualifies as a magical moment. The image is paired with patterned papers with delicate motifs. The heartfelt journaling details the importance of the season. A rub-on, a fabric label and a festive piece of silver elastic are used on the black library pocket created for the title and journaling.

"

Christmas was always such a magical time for me as a child—the lights, the decorations, the anticipation, and time with family....We hope you will always feel a sense of magic at the holidays like we did as kids and have fun things to look forward to that we do as a family...

Heather Crawford

"

Heather Crawford

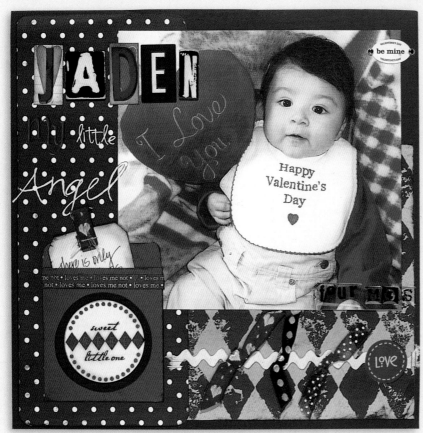

Christina Padilla

Jaden

What a little cherub, but despite the infant's enormous appeal, this Valentine's Day page might have been less sweet if the artist had printed the photo on regular photo paper. Instead, she printed the image on textured cardstock, creating the illusion that the photo is a canvas portrait. Striking harlequin and polka-dot patterned papers support the photo. Decorative ribbons, a chipboard coaster, wooden title letters, rub-ons, rickrack and more complete a layout that is lovely.

purple fleece from head
to toe,
make-up face.

trick-or-treating
door-to-door,
giving out compliments on
pumpkins

she was...

HAPPY
HALLOWEEN

Hizzy hizzy Purple Kitty Cat

2003

Ashley Calder

Purple Kitty Cat

Hizzy Hizzy Purple Kitty Cat was this little feline's name for her Halloween character. The phrase inspired the perfect title for this perfect page. The large title word is supported by multihued and multifont letter stickers. The journaling block is made by drybrushing textured cardstock with acrylic paint and then sanding it. Once dry, the edges are inked. A sassy black trim and a few colorful buttons make the purr-fect embellishments for the page.

+Q
a

Halloween trick-or-treating takes place in the evening. How do I set my child in the nighttime scene and still get a good photo?

Flash is the easy answer. If your camera allows, try "bouncing" the flash off a white ceiling. This will soften the harsh light of the flash.

Wag the Dog

From both back and front this pup is utterly adorable. The success of this simple layout depends on the quality of the photos and the interesting angle on the "rear side" picture. Simple embellishments and a wedge-shaped journaling block support without competing for attention.

Q + a

How can I prevent stark shadows from ruining my photos?

Don't prevent them. Use them! The shadows can add drama to a shot and help establish the time of day. If you just can't work with a shadow, use your camera's "fill-flash" feature to add enough light to "fill" in those shadows.

Ann Hetzel Gunkel

Coconut Cake

Devoting a layout to foods traditionally served at holiday gatherings is a wonderful way to scrapbook the holidays. Support images of your special dish with photos printed in both sepia and color. Create a stitched blocked background of patterned papers. Add tags embellished with ribbons, buttons and charms. The crowning touch is the recipe itself!

Mary MacAskill

A Christmas Pretzel

Take one terrific photograph. Add a pocket with great journaling and a compelling black-and-white photo. Put them together on a digital scrapbook page, and you've got a dish!

+Q a

How do I make my own food look as appetizing as images in magazines?

Use natural light whenever possible. Make the focus of your image the surface and texture for a mouth-watering image. And be a realist, it's just about impossible to make a bowl of mush *look* tasty.

Ann Hetzel Gunkel

Some of Daddy & Mama's favorite memories are of the sights and smells of childhood Swieconka. Now we rejoice in our chance to share this with you. We hope someday you will treasure your heritage and keep these customs dear.
Ann Hetzel Gunkel

Polish Easter Basket

Swieconka is one of the most enduring and beloved Polish traditions. The basket of goodies, which is part of the holiday, serves as one of the focal photos for this spread. Clever labeling of the basket's contents serves as journaling. This digitally created page includes papers, tag, tab and staples all designed with a computer.

Ann Hetzel Gunkel

Traditional and Less Traditional Palettes

Push the boundaries of accepted holiday color combinations for stunning results

Here comes Santa Claus dressed from head to toe in his traditional fuzzy red outfit! And after he's retired to the North Pole to begin to compile next year's "naught and nice" list, scrapbookers break out their red (and green) papers to scrapbook their favorite Christmas photos. And while red is always a hot Christmas color, why not consider some equally exciting palettes for your ho-ho-ho pictures?

Sharing

When you are in the military and far from your family during the holidays, it can be very lonely. When Dad's ship was docked in Villefrance during Christmas 1951, they had the opportunity to make Christmas very merry for a group of orphans. The children were invited onto the ship for a holiday feast along with gifts and the chance to play on a huge ship. Dad often talks about the little ones running around on deck with huge turkey legs in their hands. This picture touches my heart each time I look at it. Such a small gesture on the part of the sailors made a huge impact on these children.

CHRISTMAS

Villefrance, France 1951

Dana Zarling

Sharing Christmas

The holidays are and always have been about sharing. This heritage photo of a sailor docked in France in 1951 warms the heart of his family today. Scrapbooked on a layout predominantly created with patterned red paper, the black-and-white photo seems almost dream like. Journaling and snowflake embellishments complete the layout.

CHRISTMAS CAROLS MAKE GREAT PAGE TITLES

Stop racking your brain for just the right page title for your Christmas layout. Just whistle a happy tune and let the song title become your page title as well.

Oh Christmas Tree	Santa Claus is Coming to Town!
It's Beginning to Look a Lot Like Christmas	Joy to the World!
Deck the Halls With Boughs of Holly	May Your Days Be Merry and Bright
I'm Dreaming of a White Christmas	I'll Be Home for Christmas
We Wish You a Merry Christmas	Ho, Ho, Ho Who Would Know?
Let It Snow!	Star of Wonder, Star of Light
Chestnuts Roasting on an Open Fire	Walking in a Winter Wonderland

Shine

The Christmas tree in the photo is decorated with primitive folk-art ornaments, and that primitive feeling is carried into the cream and ivory layout. A quote is stitched to the inked fabric background with embroidery floss. Buttons border the page. Muslin and lace decorate the rustic heart and star next to a photo mat trimmed with scallop-edged scissors. A title tag trimmed with twine completes the unusual layout.

Ashley Calder

Theresa Lundström

Rudolf?

This artist had the good fortune to get a special visitor near the holidays. The majestic creature is captured with a zoom lens. For the layered background, each block of paper is softly torn. To re-create the look, dab water onto paper edges and tear along the damp line.

Most of my photographs taken in snowy conditions are either too dark or too bright. What is going on?

You have all this very white reflective stuff (aka snow) and a dark something in the middle (aka your child in a snowsuit). Your camera takes these two extremes and averages them so that nothing looks good. To avoid this, fill the frame with your subject so less of the bright snow is visible in the scene.

Hippity Hoppity Pastel Pages

Pastel is perfect for Easter pages, but when your stash of pale pinks, blues, yellows and greens run low, you may wish to reach for some of your other papers to create unusual and beautiful Easter layouts.

Melanie Douthit

Easter

Visions of chocolate bunnies and marshmallow treats are dancing in front of the eyes of this cutie. The colorful photos are scrapbooked on a traditional palette of gentle pastels. A floral embellished tag and ribbons add a celebratory flavor to the festive layout.

Egg-Hunting

Layouts that immortalize a child's glee are irresistible. When the black-and-white photo is spot colored and scrapbooked on an interesting palette of pastels, primaries and earth tones, it just can't be beat. The photo is matted on a stitched green frame. Additional stitching is used on both borders and blocked page elements. A tiny tag and a charm hang from a floral brad in the middle of big bold flowers.

Birgit Koopsen

Hunt Is On

Boisterous primary colors charge this Easter page with the energy of a toddler on a quest for goodies! Textured cardstocks form the background, photo mats and wavy title strip. Metallic alphabet letters join the stamped title. The palette is pulled together with a colorful slide mount, page reinforcers and ribbon.

Virginia Dee Williams

“ *At first Ty wanted to open each egg and eat the contents before moving on to the next egg. With a little encouragement and a sucker in his mouth we were able to convince him to pick up the rest of the eggs and put them in his basket!* ”

Virginia Dee Williams

Hurray for the Red, White and Blue

Fourth of July parades are red, white and blue from one end to the other, and the palette works perfectly for holiday pages celebrating America's birthday. But throw in a few other colors, and see what happens to your Independence Day layouts! Flag-waving fun!

Summer Ford

American Beauty

Independence Day proved a thought-provoker for this artist. As she saw her young daughter in a patriotic bikini, she felt peace in knowing that her daughter would grow up in a free country where she can "dream big and achieve anything." Printed transparencies are mounted on layers of stitched and painted paper. The painted photo frame is created by lightly tracing around the photo, removing the image and painting upon the background along the traced lines. The image is then mounted in place. A slide mount, ribbons and flowers embellish the red, white and blue layout.

Pint-sized Patriot

The focus of this great page stays on the focal photo because of clever cropping and framing with patterned and solid papers. The support photo and torn white page element are adorned with tiny heart brads. Ribbons wave merrily along the edge of the support photo.

Cheryl Baase

America

Red, white, blue, PURPLE and YELLOW all over defines the palette for this patriotic page. Movement is created with the use of horizontal lines. A journaled transparency covers the yellow section of the layout. Strips of mesh, swirl clips, fibers, a large stencil letter, a tiny bookplate, stars, a word plaque and a bracelet of word charms carry on the America-the-beautiful theme.

Sheila Riddle

" I love to focus on the photo. When my cousin took this picture of my daughter, Baylee, I knew it was a one-photo layout!
Sheila Riddle *"*

Melanie Douthit

Born in the USA

This artist scrapbooked her child's first Independence Day on this lovely layout. Her journaling reflects deeply about the tragedy that struck America on 9/11. Key words within the text are accented by an increase in point size. The background consists of layers of patterned paper. Patriotic-themed bottle caps, brads, stickers, ribbon and rub-on title letters contribute to the page.

Traditional Halloween Colors

Crunchy leaves and pumpkins help define the Halloween palette that most often comes to mind. But other colors can be drawn from costumes and skin tones (and the corners of our imaginations) and make our Halloween layouts quirky and equally memorable.

A Girl and Her Dog

Orange and black are traditional Halloween colors, and the ripped blue paper works beautifully to accent the palette. Photos of these cross-dressers dominate the humorous page. (This is the third year for the model and dog team to dress in these costumes and sadly, the artist says, it will be the last, because the human model will be too big for her fur next year.) A collection of tags and embellishments adds weight to the upper corner of the focal photo.

> *I enjoy scrapbooking the holidays as a way to document changes. It's a way to see how much my child has changed in a year.*
> Mary Hager

Mary Hager

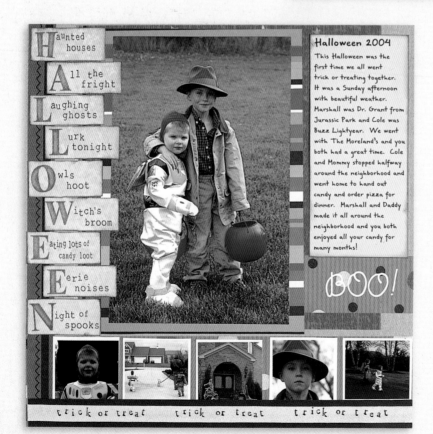

Susan Kondrat

Halloween 2004

This layout documents the first time this family went trick-or-treating together, and the happy palette captures the fun of the experience. The journaling border on the left side of the page is adhered in a funky jig-jag pattern. A photo border at the page bottom and the journaling block on the right side of the layout frame the focal image of two buds out for the loot.

Laura McKinley

Stinker

Pink may be an unusual color to use on a Halloween layout and an even more unique color choice for a "boy" page, but this layout proves that it works beautifully. The color picks up the model's warm skin and lip tones and adds a note of irony to the artwork. The papers are distressed with acrylic paint. The title and ornate details are stamped using paint and foam stamps.

OVERLOOKED HOLIDAY PAGE THEMES

Looking for some new holiday page ideas? Why not scrapbook some not-often-scrapbooked events?

Christmas
• Gift shopping
• Letters to Santa
• Christmas parades

Thanksgiving
• Favorite stuffing recipes
• Lists of things you are most thankful for
• Centerpieces throughout the years

Hanukkah
• Latke-making and Bubbie's favorite recipe
• Collections of menorahs and dreidels

Valentine's Day
• The creation of the school "card box"
• Cards from throughout the years
• Favorite love poems and songs
• Photos of your first crushes to current flames

Kwanzaa
• Favorite songs
• Shopping for the decorations
• Family tree and history

Halloween
• Making costumes
• Getting ready for trick-or-treating
• The haul of candy

Handcrafted Gift Sets

Use a few scrapbook supplies to create personalized gifts for the holidays

Giving a homemade gift speaks volumes to the recipient. It shows that someone thinks about a certain person so much that she took time and creativity to create something truly unique. Here are a few holiday gift ideas that require no more than four simple supplies (paper, stamps, ink and ribbon) and a computer to create.

Heidi Schueller

Monogrammed Stationery Set

Help a friend or relative be stylishly thoughtful with a custom-created stationery set. This set includes stationery paper, thank-you cards and matching envelopes. The paper is cut from white cardstock and edged with strips of patterned paper and ribbon. The monogram is stamped. The thank-you cards and matching envelopes are created from textured cardstock and similarly embellished. When finished, cover a small gift box with the same patterned paper and add a beautiful bow of sheer ribbon.

Heidi Schueller

Personalized Gift Bags

Linen bags bulging with the dry ingredients necessary to throw together a pot of soup or a few dozen cookies make thoughtful gifts. Personalize the bags with homemade tags and labels. Punch circles of patterned paper to decorate metal-rimmed circle tags and attach to ribbon with a jump ring. For the labels, print sentiments on patterned paper and cut it into blocks. Mat with solid cardstock that has been edged with decorative scissors or border punches.

Photo CD and Decorated Cover

Are friends and relatives constantly oohing and aahing over your beautiful photos? Thank them with a personalized CD of images. Create a 4 x 4" mini page to act as the CD case cover and decorate the disk with patterned paper.

Heidi Schueller

Shining Seasonal Pages

Savor the poetry of spring, summer, fall and winter

The seasons are utterly unique. Each has its own distinct fingerprint. Spring earth smells ripe and rich as deep chocolate with just a hint of fruit rising on updrafts. Summer blisters, burns and buzzes with insects. Autumn brings the first biting breath of cold, logs burning in fireplaces and leaves crunching under foot. And winter slips in to seal the world in a slicker of blue-white ice.

As the seasons shift, so do our personal patterns and activities. We sleep later or rise earlier. We spend more or less time outside, and baseball bats are replaced by hockey sticks. Our clothing changes with the weather, and we leave behind last year's favorite snow parka to purchase a new one for our growing children.

Scrapbookers love to record the patterns of the seasons with photos and journaling. Their seasonal pages honor Mother Nature and our interactions with her. Beautiful seasonal papers are available to support the colors within the photos, and embellishments from silver snowflake charms to silk flowers are there for the picking at most any craft store.

It is a joy to scrapbook the four seasons on pages that are poetically fluid, compelling and emotional.

Shannon Taylor

"
God writes the songs that children sing,
Around the world from spring to spring.

Lois Duncan
"

Spring Fills the Air

Create fresh pages with spring photos

What is it about spring that makes our hearts lift inside our chests? Perhaps it is the feeling that as the world wakes, anything is possible. We celebrate each new bud as a miracle of nature. Scrapbook the colors of spring, from the gentle pinks of rose blossoms to the blazing yellows of daffodils on pages that make you want to sing.

Lisa Turley

Buttercups

A field of flowers framing a budding young lady is the focus of this delicious page. A palette of rich color, a stamped title, ribbons, fibers and brads join delicate stitching to frame the photos.

Song of Spring

This was a year when Spring forgot.
She stayed in the southlands far too long.
Snow lay piled on the garden path
And winter winds sang the robin's song.

When nature gave her a gentle shove
Spring set things right. In a matter of hours
She changed all the icicles into leaves,
And all the snowballs she turned to flowers.

Lois Duncan

Jane Davies

Kalamoir Spring

Spring shows its many faces in the close-up photos showcased on this delightful page. The macro focusing feature on the artist's camera allowed the artist to move in for super-tight shots. A delicate title and journaling block balance the photos. Paper squares embellish the lower border of the layout.

Spring

Spring in Sweden can be chilly and sweaters and fuzzy hats get their share of wear. But when those first buds push their way out of the ground even a brrrr day has to be embraced. Flower patterned vellum hugs the corner of this focal photo. A substantial journaling block discusses how happy this child's family is to finally own a house with their own yard.

Ulrika Ost

I'd like to write poetry to use on my scrapbook page but I get overwhelmed. I want to explain what feeling but I just don't know how. Help?

That overwhelmed feeling is often sparked when a poet tries to write about too broad of a topic. Instead of writing about "everything I love about spring," for example, focus in on a single aspect of the season, such as a flower or a moment you particularly enjoy.

Virginia Hylton Park
March 2005

So SweEt

Spring Blossoms

New Fresh

Patti Milazzo

Spring Blossoms

± **Q**
a

Patterned paper can be expensive! Do I have to use it on all my scrapbook pages?

There is no "have to" in scrapbooking, so of course you don't necessarily need to use it on all your layouts. But you may also wish to look for ways to make your patterned paper go farther. Use it to create page borders or journaling blocks and rely on cardstock for larger paper page elements.

Spring Blossoms

Subtle spot coloring of the flower in the photo makes this page especially compelling. Supporting images add shots of intense color to the page. The title is pieced together with fiber, alphabet stickers and a rub-on letter. Decorative brads, stitching, photo turns and a metal ring join a collection of flowers to complete the page.

Earth Laughs in Flowers

Floral photos adorn tags set against basket-weave paper make this spread a delight to look at. The stamped title and flower-stamped images add to the layout while the journaling block relays the artist's joy at her Maine garden's bounty.

FLOWER POWER

Flowers are a common theme in poetry and art. Different flowers are linked to different emotions or meanings. Create your own symbolic floral layout by picking the representative bloom of your choice.

- Aster: Love, daintiness
- Bluebell: Humility
- Pink carnation: I'll never forget you
- Magnolia: Nobility
- Petunia: Anger
- Rose: (red) Love, (pink) Perfect happiness, (white) I am worthy of you
- Sweetpea: Goodbye
- Tulip: Perfect lover
- Violet: Let's take a chance
- Zinnia: (white) Goodness

Cynthia Bisson

Hot Summer Scrapbook Pages

Splash and sizzle with pages that celebrate the freedom that summer brings

Turn up the air conditioner and pull out your scrapbooking supplies. It's time for a few hours of cool-down fun, scrapbooking those jump-in-the-pool and just-find-shade days of good ol' summertime.

Tia Bennett

Sign of Summer

When the weather sizzles, the flip-flops come out of the closet. As much a part of summer as Popsicles, these comfy shoes are a symbol that the school year is finally over. Showcase a closely cropped photo of flip-flops on a background of sky blue.

Katie Watson

The Last Breath of Summer

A huff and a puff and a wish is born. This spread shows the tiny seeds taking flight.
The sequence of photos are mounted on patterned paper. Tags are strung with ribbon
across the right side of the layout. Buttons and additional ribbon embellish. The patch is
hand-embroidered with a dandelion image. Journaling recalls the day by the lake and the
child's determination to set every last flower seed free for the winter.

Sunflowers

A stroke of genius—the colorizing of the yellow sunflowers
on the black-and-white photo, is
what makes this page so strong.
A tightly cropped photo of one
of the flowers is framed below.
Handmade paper, paper rope,
metal phrases and brads complete the scene.

Kristy Lee

Fresh Produce

How cute are these little peaches! With photos of a little girl as appealing as this, a scrapbook spread is sure to be a winner. The photos are mounted on summery patterned papers. A stamped title and a journaling block that includes metal tags tell the story of a day at the produce market. Ribbon and brads complete the spread.

Song of Summer

Wealth of summer,
Dreamers' gold—
For so short a time
It is mine to hold.
Gold in the meadow,
Gold on the hill,
Slanted light when
The world is still;
Golden currency,
Mine to spend,
Here where the sun-
Warmed grasses bend,
That shining glory
Beyond compare—
So warm and molten
Upon my hair.

Lois Duncan

Katie Watson

Splash

And the competition is on! Who can make the biggest splash? These little guys have the results documented in these great photos. Sticker letters form the title. A fiber-tied tag holds journaling. Delicate stitching ties the page elements together seamlessly.

Tyler and his cousin, Brandonlee enjoyed every chance to pose for photos. The pool was their favorite place to smile and show off their talents.

ONE, TWO, THREE.........JUMP!
Spring Break San Diego Style!

MAR 2005

Tracy Weinzapfel Burgos

Ashley Calder

This Place

This place is magical. It is silent and filled with the smells of blooming flowers. This place is special and deserves to be scrapbooked and remembered forever. The photo is mounted on a background of rose cardstock. The cardstock is painted white, sanded, cut into segments and stitched. The stems and leaves are painted. Silk flowers are embellished with buttons.

+Q a

Is "handmade paper" really handmade?

It can be. Some scrapbook artists enjoy the process of making their own paper, throwing in flower petals and other things to make it utterly unique. But most scrapbookers rely on manufactured papers that have the same rustic look and feeling and are called "handmade."

Capturing the Flavors of Fall

Ignite scrapbook pages with the warmth of earth tones

Crunchy autumn leaves and orange pumpkins define both the most common color palettes and most common themes for fall pages. But look for accent colors to add pop to your pages and papers with texture. Pull out your sewing machine and stitch page elements together to create pages warm enough to snuggle with.

Vicki Boutin

Peekaboo Fall

This page is all about the photo, and the artist is careful to keep the attention on it. Strips of patterned papers form a background under the image. Charms, stamps, stickers and other alphabet embellishments form the title. The decorative frame is placed over label tape directly above the inked journaling block.

Fall Song

It's autumn, and the leaves grow old.
Their vibrant green turns rust and gold
And finally brown. The wind comes by
To soothe them with a lullaby.

They flutter to the song she sings
And drop like birds with heavy wings
To settle in a weary heap
And crackle once then fall asleep.

Lois Duncan

Nancy Boyle

Great Smoky Mountains

Supplies that bring the textures and colors of nature create a rustic atmosphere for these outdoor photos. Decorative tags wrapped with ribbons and fibers join large chipboard letters, label-tape journaling and swatches of fraying fabric on a spread that's likely to make the most avid homebody want to get out and hike.

Emily

Poetry is used to journal this fetching fall layout. Brads hold the journaled transparency in place beneath a dazzling color photo. Tiny stamped tags hang from a delicate stretch of fiber.

Sara Bryans

Apple-Picking Day

Rustic burlap makes itself at home on a background of patterned papers on this great layout. The same burlap is stitched into pockets for journaling. A patterned paper strip and a title tag carry the apple-picking theme. Tags, brads, safety pins, buttons, a bookplate and hemp form collaged elements.

 What a perfect day we had for picking apples! This is a big family event every year!...We picked a huge bag just for the three of us and made apple pies the following day.

Melodee Langworthy

Melodee Langworthy

Fall

A cozy quilted background of patterned papers and cardstock are stitched together to support this fall photo. Stamped and embossed leaves decorate select blocks, and journaling and a sticker title lend weight to others.

Lonni McMullen

Lisa Turley

Simple Fall Fun

While this fall page celebrating the simple joys of a haystack romp looks difficult to create, it is very can-do. The patterned paper strips and blocks are mounted on black cardstock before being mounted on the background. Metallic ribbons are tucked behind one of the matted strips at the top of the page. Metallic fall-themed stickers embellish and metallic watercolors add a bit more gleam to the photo mat. Rub-ons form the page title.

FROM WHITHER COMETH INSPIRATION?

Poets have penned verses about everything imaginable. Open yourself up to be stimulated by the world around you.

- Take time to sniff. The smells surrounding us evoke strong feelings, often bringing back memories.

- Listen to music. Songs inspire feelings and link us to events that took place when certain tunes were popular.

- Look through your closet. Touch the clothing. Try to remember when and where you bought it and why. On what special occasions have you worn it?

- Look at your photos and revisit the moments they were taken.

- Return to locations you haven't visited in years. Let yourself remember what it was like "back then."

Wonderful Winter Wonderland Pages

Wrap up snowy winter memories on beautiful layouts

Button up your overcoat and brave the outdoors just long enough to snap photos of your favorite folks frolicking in the snow. These photos of good times will find warm receptions on scrapbook pages. Cool blue and green palettes work well with winter photos, but don't forget to heat things up a bit with some primary elements!

Martha Crowther

Winter Song

What is springtime? Nothing now.
All the streams are frozen still.
Snow lies heavy on the land.
Nothing stirs upon the hill.

What is springtime? Nothing now.
Still there is the faintest sound,
Whispering beneath the earth—
Laughter deep in frozen ground.

Lois Duncan

Snow

These fantastic black-and-white photos capture the biting cold of a winter's day. But not even freezing temperatures can keep this bold boy from enjoying the snow. Scrapbooked on a text-patterned background of cool blue, the die-cut title letters and ribbon-strung journaling tag visually pop off of the page.

Burr

"But Mom, I can't MOVE!" Never mind, this cutie is appropriately bundled up against the cold, and it makes a darling photo. The gray background underscores the temperature. Die cuts spell out the title. Eyelet snow charms, brads and festive ribbons support the wintry theme.

Missy Neal

Baby It's Cold Outside

It may be cold outside but this artist knows how to heat things up on her page with bright yellow, red and orange. Chipboard letters mounted at tipped angles join rub-on letters and alphabet beads to create the fun title. Frothy fibers and ribbons help frame the photo.

Patti Hozack

Brrrr!

Cool, cool colors support these very cool photos of a boy at play. The edges of the photos are sanded and paper elements are inked for a softer effect. The stamped title, punched paper circles and squares, brads and silver snow flake provide an assortment of shapes that keep the page from becoming too linear.

Michelle Klein

Snow Buds

Friendship is a solid thing, and this chunky title formed with die-cut letters says just that. Pictures of these two outdoor mates are mounted on a background of patterned papers. Rustic decorative brads, ribbon, staples and an inked journaling block are the ice-ing on this page.

Lisa Sanders

Snow Daphne

All together now: "Ahhhhh!" This pup is doing its best to stay warm on a chilly day. Paint splattered on a cardstock background creates a snowy-looking base for this photo. Playfully ripped patterned papers, a coordinating tag, decorative brads and an enormous bow find a place on the layout. Journaling is hidden under the hinged photo.

Pam Callaghan

Snow

This page is all about balance and contrast. The viewer's eye moves easily from sepia photos to color. Each embellishment and journaling block is carefully placed to add to the layout. Decorative brads anchor the photo border. Stickers embellish. The fluffy mulberry paper seems snowlike against the pale green background.

Carrie Postma

Savvy and Seasonal Digital Art

Create a real sense of the seasons on scrapbook pages with digital art

Everyone has a favorite season, whether it involves the crackle of leaves under foot, snowflakes on eyelashes, the scent of budding flowers on the breeze, or the throb of the hot sun against the back of your neck. Use digital techniques to enhance the sights, smells, tastes, touches and sounds of the seasons for your scrapbook artwork.

we received so many nice baby gifts when you were born, but I think this one was my favorite. A little plaid hunting coat and hat that the Lewallens had made especially for you by a woman in Tulsa. It fit perfectly as you approached your first birthday, and I thought you were the cutest little guy ever in your red coat, black mittens and that little Elmer Fudd hat.

made with love

coat tales

Susan Cyrus

Cozy Paper

This warm and cozy flannel background is made by scanning the coat worn by the model in the photo at a resolution of 1200 dpi. The image is enlarged and cropped. Once printed onto photo paper, it is trimmed with pinking shears and stitched to the background paper.

Susan Cyrus

Photo-realistic Title

Look to your photo and image-editing software to create a unique page title. Open the photo in your image-editing software. Create a new layer and type the title. Select all of the letters, and turn off the title layer while activating the photo layer. Make sure the background, not the title, is selected and delete it. Your colorful title should remain. Print, trim with a craft knife and add the title to your page.

Photo Vignette

The three-photo series in the bottom right of this page is an excellent way to include more photos on the page. By colorizing the images, you can create a collection that does not distract from the focal image.

Susan Cyrus

Wonderful Wedding Pages

Design and decorate exquisite "I Do" layouts

Every little girl knows how the story ends: "And they got married and lived happily ever after." We moved from our childhood fantasies into adulthood but continued to dream about our own Prince Charming. If we are very lucky, we find him. He proposes. We say "yes." And the fairy tale ends in a beautiful wedding. Sigh.

Because weddings are so very special, they are one of the more photographed occasions in our lives. Whether the bride, groom, wedding party and trappings are shot by a professional or a friend, the images need to be scrapbooked on pages that are as lovely as the event.

Draw your palette from the wedding colors or look beyond the flowers and bridesmaid dresses to the ocean backdrop behind the gazebo, or the jewel tones in the church's stained-glass windows. Select embellishments that are premade or use bits and pieces of lace and rice to decorate your pages. Make sure you journal about the day's events and your hopes and dreams for the future.

Sara Wise

Symbols and History of Weddings

Something old—the symbols and traditions that make weddings an event

Weddings are surrounded by wonderful old traditions, and while most modern brides have no idea where they began, they find themselves joyfully clasping vintage family necklaces around their necks and tying blue ribbons around garters before the ceremony. These traditions that seem a bit mysterious actually had fascinating roots, and understanding them can make the inclusion even more fun.

Jennifer Wright, Photos: Gary Apodaca

The Elements

A dreamy wedding involves a lot of decisions and a lot of work. When the pieces come together in synchrony, a bride can relax and just enjoy the special day. This layout focuses on many of the aspects of an elegant wedding: the flowers, the goblet, the musician, the program. The journaling recounts the significance of each of the elements shown in the photos mounted on purple cardstock.

Do most people throw out "extra" photos?

Some certainly do. Others find creative ways to use those pictures that aren't going to be framed or featured as focal photos on scrapbook pages. Consider saving "extra" photos for jewelry-making, creating collages on top of jewelry boxes or using them in photo montages.

The Veil

A vintage veil adorns a new bride in the photo on this beautiful layout. The veil's original owner is seen in a photo underneath the vellum journaling block. A stretch of tulle, ribbon, ornate metal photo corners and a tiny tag embellish the page.

"

Gliding down the aisle, the bride was a vision of loveliness for all to see. Tears blurred my sight, for there in my heart it was then I recalled when the face under the veil was me.

Cathy Lucas

"

Vintage Lace

In the far back shelves of my bedroom closet, is an old lace dress and veil. For thirty years in the dark my hopes with the tulle did lay, that a daughter might wear it someday.
Three handsome sons did I birth with this groom from my youth. Sooner than expected my babies were grown and went out into this world. Then into our lives the youngest son brought Jackie, sweet, beautiful and loving, soon to be the wife that he sought.
Two years later she revealed to me, the dress for their wedding that was quickly to be. She glowed with excitement as she slipped the white satin over her head. Quietly she asked "Do you like what you see?" In earnest I replied "It's beautiful, just like you ... Matthew will be delighted, but where is your veil?" There wasn't one yet it seemed. My heart jumped with anticipation, could it be true that not for a daughter but a daughter to be, the now vintage lace veil was waiting to be used?
Gliding down the aisle, the bride was a vision of loveliness for all to see. Tears blurred my sight, for there in my heart it was then I recalled when the face under the veil was me.

Veil

Cathy Lucas

I can still remember how the breeze felt on my skin. I was so nervous to walk down the aisle because I kept tripping over my dress. When I got up to the gazebo Pastor Zaviengo was so soothing. Then Jonathan grabbed my hand and I felt so secure. From then on it was just right... Everything our pastor said was so moving, my soon to be husband looked so handsome, there were tears of joy, and it didn't rain!! I could not get the smile off of my face. Even though I couldn't get the Unity Candle to light, when Jonathan lit it, I knew I would be taken care of forever. After we exchanged rings, I realized the ceremony was almost over, and pretty soon I would be Mrs Contes... I was so excited. To hear the words, "I now pronounce you husband and wife" was just amazing. It was a perfect moment.

The Bride

A monochromatic cream palette and the glow surrounding this bride's veil make her appear almost surreal in this series of photos. The quick and elegant layout requires no embellishment. The journaling and photos supply all the pow factor needed to carry the layout.

glow (glo) I. to give off a bright light 2. to be elated 3. a countenance that reflects great joy

Kristina Contes, Photo: Daniel S. Krieger

White Wedding Dress

Throughout history brides donned their very best gowns for their weddings. These gowns varied in color, depending upon both the traditions of their times and the clothing they had in their wardrobes. But in 1499, Anne of Brittany, Queen of France, wore a beautiful white wedding dress for her ceremony. Admiration for Queen Anne had brides around the world imitating her fashion style, and the tradition of wearing a white wedding gown continues to this day.

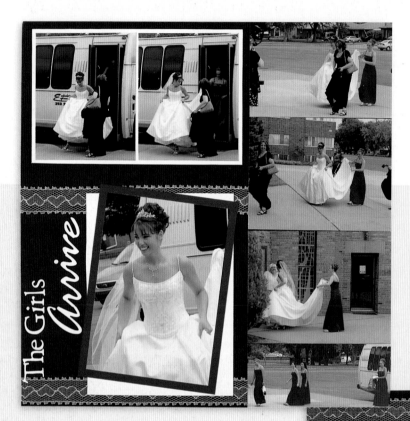

The Girls Arrive

A series of photos showing the bridal party arriving at the church are scrapbooked on black cardstock. A hot red photo mat frames the focal photo, picking up on the color of the bridesmaids' gowns. Decorative heart lace and several heart-shaped tags embellish the spread.

Q+a

How do I keep a layout with a black background from looking too stark?

Allow the black to provide the drama for your layout. You provide dimension with clean white photo mats and other small page elements. Including a hot accent color gives the page energy.

Emily Murray, Photos: Samantha Cover of A Thousand Words Photography

Man on the Right

It was a groom's job to protect his bride from those who might wish to set upon them, kidnapping her or stealing her possessions. In order to best protect his bride, he held his sword in his right hand and had to place himself on her right side. The bride and groom maintained this position throughout the ceremony.

Syalynne Kramer, Photos: Gary Rowley

The Ceremony

The vows taken by the bride and groom are captured in this series of photos. While the images themselves are stunning, the deep turquoise background is what makes the layout work so well, complementing the water behind the couple. Metal embellishments, including word washers, embellish the page. Flowers cut from patterned paper and chipboard title letters complete the spread.

WAY BACK WHEN: SOMETHING BLUE

The color blue was long considered the color of holiness. Out of that concept grew the idea that a bride should wear a band of blue around the hem of her wedding gown. That band morphed over the years, and brides more often began wearing a blue garter. Today's brides may choose to fulfill the old tradition by wearing a piece of blue jewelry, blue ribbons in their hair, or even a spiffy blue tattoo.

I can still remember how the breeze felt on my skin. I was so nervous to walk down the aisle because I kept tripping over my dress. When I got up to the gazebo Pastor Zarlengo was so soothing. Then Jonathan grabbed my hand and I felt so secure. From then on it was just right...

Kristina Contes

The Bridal Party and Witnesses

While many marriages were tidily arranged, sometimes the bride's family didn't look favorably on proposed marriage alliances. When the groom was not to be put off, he might decide to kidnap his bride-to-be and carry her back to his own lands to be wed. This risky escapade called for help from a best friend or "best man." And the bride-to-be needed protection during her journey and ladies to attend to her needs. These "bride's maids" provided both. Family attending the ceremony supported the bride and helped the day run smoothly.

Linda Garrity

Three Friends

This photo tells the story of three friends who have supported each other throughout their growing-up years and now support each other as their lives together change. The image is scrapbooked on pink and ivory patterned papers. A flutter of ribbons borders the photo.

My Family

Special events bring families together, and photos recording the event remind everyone of the closeness they share. This bride and her family are featured on a stitched and inked mat. Patterned papers form the background for the layout. Journaling strips and a journaled circle tell the bride's story.

Linda Sobolewski

Heather Burch, Photo: Robert Burch

WAY BACK WHEN: THE OFFICIATE

Historically, marriages did not have to be officiated by a member of the clergy in order to be considered legal and binding. All that was necessary was for the bride and groom to declare their intention to be man and wife in front of witnesses. In some places, the bride and groom were "handfasted," which involved the joining of hands and the declaration that they intended to live as man and wife for a year and a day. After that period of time, they could either renew their handfast or officially decide to make the union permanent.

Thank You, Mom

Behind every good woman there is a great mother. This bride took the time to thank her mother for all she contributed to the bride's life. The creative layout includes flattened antique silver spoons (representing the fact that both the bride and her mother enjoy antiques). The journaling block combines lined paper, a "happiness card" and tags. The large flower embellishment dominates the page, insisting that the layout be upbeat, and the playful ribbons support the message.

The Flowers

Originally, brides carried bouquets made up of herbs and grains that were believed to have magical powers. A bride might carry garlic to ward off evil spirits, sage to gain wisdom or dill to conjure up lusty feelings. Over time, these bouquets changed to include flowers. The flowers themselves were then linked to mystical and magical powers.

Suzy Plantamura

Flowers

This stunning bridal photo is scrapbooked on text patterned paper. A photo of a bridal flower is enlarged and mounted below the transparent journaling block. Supporting images of flowers adorning the wedding cake and used as center pieces on tables are mounted and embellished with tiny silk flowers. More tiny flowers are sprinkled over the page title.

DON'T-MISS PHOTO MOMENTS

Traditionally, wedding photos include shots of the bride in her gown, the wedding party, close-ups of the couple's clenched hands and the first dance. But there are other events that are wonderful to record in photos:

- Shopping for the ring, bridal gown, invitations and cake
- Shopping for and the registering of china and silver, etc.
- Getting hair and nails done
- Bachelor and bachelorette parties
- Piles of wedding gifts
- Making of the centerpieces, decoration of the church and reception hall
- Quiet moments of contemplation before the wedding
- Behind-the-scenes preparations of the wedding party before the march
- The faces of the bride's and groom's parents during the ceremony
- The musicians
- The decoration of the get-away vehicle
- After-reception cleanup

Syalynne Kramer

A Very Beautiful Bride

All brides are beautiful because they radiate happiness. This bride beams from her wedding photos like a magazine model. The images are scrapbooked on a background of patterned paper and green textured cardstock. The pink journaling block and chipboard title block draw their shade from the patterned paper. Tiny flowers create a border that connects the three photos.

Flower Girls

These beautiful flower girls are showcased on a digitally created layout that features digital ribbons and flowers. Originally, the photo background behind the young models was too busy and distracting, so the artist selectively darkened the area.

WAY BACK WHEN: FLOWER GIRLS

Originally, flower girls were maidens whose job it was to walk in front of the bride as she made her way toward the groom. They scattered herbs and grains that would protect her, keeping evil spirits away, until she was safely in the protection of her husband.

Doris Castle

The Wedding Cake

The earliest known wedding cakes were actually loaves of bread that the groom broke over his bride's head as a sign of both dominance and fertility. That tradition gave way to another in which small cakes were stacked, and the bride and groom were required to kiss over the tower. If they managed to do this without tipping over the cakes, they were ensured fertility and good luck. These early wedding cakes were simple sweets, and it wasn't until much later that iced palaces finally became popular.

The cake is such an overlooked part of the reception -- almost an afterthought. And yet, the artistry that goes into making the cake takes great skill and vision. The beauty of the cake usually reflects the taste and beauty of the bride herself. From the delicate marzipan flowers to the light and airy frosting -- each element gives grace and elegance that cannot be denied.

Amy Goldstein

The Cake

A cake this frothy and detailed can stand alone on a clean white background with only a few well-selected embellishments. A sprinkle of delicate blue flowers features tiny rhinestones centers. More rhinestones decorate a harlequin paper embellishment strip.

Love

A delicate patterned paper background is embellished with stunning embossed paper accents. The title letters are sprayed with a product that simulates stone. Rustic brads hold down inked photo corners. The handwritten journaling block details the bride's memories of her wedding reception.

How do I make glass-like embellishments for my pages?

Cut paper shapes into your desired sizes. Cover the shapes entirely with watermark ink and then add three layers of embossing powder. Once dry, put the accents in your freezer for a few minutes. When cool, remove and gently bend the accents until cracks appear.

Samantha Walker, Photos; Rita Walker

The Kiss

While the origins of kissing are unknown, experts speculate that the practice emerged from a desire to sniff another's scent. Others speculate that a kiss is actually the sharing of breath—a symbol that those involved are sharing something essential to life. In Roman times a kiss was considered the sealing of a bond or contract. Today, the kiss between a bride and groom seals the marriage vows.

Reaction to the Kiss

You must remember this: a kiss is still a kiss...go the lyrics to the old song. But a wedding kiss is even more special, as seen by the reaction of the bride and her court in this photo. The image is scrapbooked on a black cardstock background. Delicate purple flower shapes and a beaded bracelet form a border across the bottom of the page. The support photo is framed with elegant silver photo corners.

Gracie Ortiz, Photo: Danny L. Flores

WEDDING MEMORABILIA TO SCRAPBOOK

Weddings come with oodles of trappings including the tiered cake, bridal bouquet and engraved goblets. While these pieces of memorabilia are far too bulky to include on your scrapbook pages, there are many other mementos that can be easily scrapbooked including:

- The wedding announcement
- The wedding invitation
- Caterer, band, DJ, bakery and florist cards
- Brochures from considered service and reception locations
- Tags and receipts from wedding attire
- The guest list
- Hair pins and hair ornaments used by the bride

- The rehearsal dinner menu
- Sheet music of songs performed during the ceremony
- Gift cards, wrapping paper and ribbon from presents
- A bit of lace from the veil
- The garter
- A flower from the bouquet and the groom's boutonnière
- Pieces of rice
- Honeymoon brochures and keepsakes

Fashion and Trends

Something new—times change and brides change right along with them

The "new" in the old rhyme refers to the fact that a bride is entering into a new and exciting phase of her life. But for today's brides, the "new" can mean any number of things. Modern women are taking charge of their own lives. They are defining their love lives, their vows and bringing their own personalities to their weddings.

I had broken my leg skiing a week prior to February 14th and I was home sitting in my chair being bored and completely ready to go back to work and do something other than sit around the house.

Jeffrey and I were laying about on that Sunday evening and nothing was on the television that remotely appealed to either of us. While channel surfing, I jokingly put on an old episode of the Walton's entitled "The Wedding" and said to Jeff, "Look it's John-Boy and his girlfriend!" During this episode John boy had a spat with his fiancée and broken off a previous engagement and was about to re-propose to her. It was a typical marriage proposal and he had gotten down on bended knee and asked he to marry him – again.

In his usual somewhat sarcastic manner, Jeffrey leaned over to me and said "What would you do if I asked you to marry me like that?" To which I replied, "Yea, right!! Like you would ask that.". He then pleaded, "No really!" My reply was "Sure, right, in a New York Minute!"

Without a missing a beat he reached into his pocket and pulled out a gorgeous antique 2 caret ring and got on his knee and asked "Will you marry me?" I was laughing and crying in all the same moment. Eventually after the hysterics subsided I said yes.

He didn't want to ask me to marry him on Valentines Day because that was his father's birthday and he had planned to ask me at dinner the night I had broken my leg skiing so I had foiled all of his best laid plans.

So ultimately, I was proposed to in a pair of shorts and a sweatshirt with my leg in a plaster cast with the Walton's on the television in the background and I would have to say it was the MOST ROMANTIC proposal EVER!

a happy heart makes the face cheerful. PROVERBS 15:13

the Proposal happiness

Amy Goldstein

The Proposal

A beaming bride recalls the events that made her proposal memorable in the extensive journaling block on this page. Minimal embellishing, including epoxy word pebbles and a simple frame, complete the layout.

Ultimately, I was proposed to in a pair of shorts and a sweatshirt with my leg in a plaster cast with 'The Walton's' on the television in the background and I would have to say it was the MOST ROMANTIC proposal EVER!

Amy Goldstein

WAY BACK WHEN: PROPOSALS

Only recently have grooms been "brazenly forward" enough to propose directly to the woman they wish to marry. Historically, proposals of marriage were treated as business meetings in which a man would travel, or send a representative, to the home of his future bride. The parties would meet and negotiations would take place to iron out issues such as the bride's dowry. It is said that, should the groom's traveling party pass a blind man, a monk or a pregnant woman, it boded ill for the future marriage but if they passed a wolf or a goat, the marriage was to be blessed.

I Now Pronounce You Husband and Wife

Cream and brown cardstocks and patterned papers support a photo of the bride and groom, a meaningful journaling block and an altered CD on this lovely layout. The CD is painted with acrylic paints, sanded and then rub-on flowers are placed on top. The lyrical journaling above the CD holds the musical theme together.

Leanne Reist-Barr, Photos: Troy Algar

Bridal Ink

Yesterday's brides were more shy than overt but today's brides feel comfortable letting it all hang out. Being a grown woman is knowing who you are and letting others know you as well. This bride has no problem with the concept. Her gown displays the tattoo on her back boldly, and she frames the photo in jewel-like flowers and brads to draw the eyes to the image. Patterned papers create wedge-shaped backgrounds, and a white textured cardstock journaling block brings the bride's voice to the layout.

WAY BACK WHEN: MAN AND WIFE

Because a woman was considered the property of her husband, without rights or even the ability to own lands, earlier vows most often included the phrase "I now pronounce you man and wife." However today's brides often prefer the phrase "I now pronounce you husband and wife" because of the parity between the two words which indicates equality in the union.

Megan Dorfan, Photo: Frank Melo

Create a Wedding Theme Album

Go for ease and cohesion when creating a wedding album

The aftermath of weddings most often includes huge amounts of extra cake, discarded embossed paper and...photos! Lots and lots of photos! You may wish to scrapbook each image on a page that is distinct and different from all others. Or you may wish to create a theme album. Theme albums are unique because they draw a design concept from page to page. As a result, the album looks and reads as if it is a self-contained book.

Jessie Baldwin, Photos: Anthony Masters

What greater thing is there for two human souls that to feel that they are joined together to strengthen each other in all labour, to minister to each other in all sorrow, to share with each other in all gladness, to be one with each other in the silent unspoken memories?

George Eliot

Keep Patterns to a Minimum

A strong theme album begins with the collection of a handful of papers that work well together. These may include prints in various sizes as well as solids. The unifying factor is most often the color palette and style of the selected papers. Color blocking with your chosen papers creates a quick background that can easily be modified for each subsequent page without abruptly changing the album's design. By stitching the blocks together on each page, the shared design concept is reinforced.

Repeat Embellishments and Accents

The pages within this wedding theme album are tied together with more than just the black-and-white palette. Embellishments also play a role in unifying the pages so that the book looks as though its design has been well considered. The black-and-white ribbon that stretches vertically across this page is also found on other pages within the album. The ornate silver photo corner, used as an embellishment on a single corner of the photo, is another repeated design element in the book.

Jessie Baldwin, Photos: Anthony Masters

Jessie Baldwin, Photos: Anthony Masters

Keep Type Styles Consistent

Typography plays an important role in unifying the pages in a wedding theme album. While point size may vary between elements and pages, the style of the fonts remains consistently elegant (or playful or bold, etc.). This page includes a beautiful page title printed on a slip of green cardstock. Similar titles appear on other pages of the book. Printed papers underscore the wedding theme and handwritten journaling adds a personal touch.

Cards and Invitations

Create cards and invitations with your scrapbook supplies

Card-making is a natural extension of scrapbooking. Using tools and supplies that are already in a scrapbooker's craft room, and many of the same skills, you can turn out cards that are much more personal than the store-bought variety. The assembly-line process of card-making makes for fast and easy invitations and announcements!

Jessie Baldwin

Quick and Easy Photo Card

This computer-generated photo card is made to be slipped into a regular envelope and mailed to guests, asking them to "save the date" of the upcoming nuptials. Use image-editing software to convert the photo to black-and-white. Add the text in layers, altering font sizes and opacity levels for interest. Crop and mount the photo onto white cardstock and embellish with a ribbon and charm. Finish by mounting the card onto red cardstock.

WAY BACK WHEN: WEDDING INVITATIONS

There is something about a wedding invitation that makes you reach for it first when sorting through the day's mail. Perhaps it is the heavy, creamy paper stock on which it is written, or the graceful and formal way it is addressed. Today's stunning invitation has evolved over the centuries. Many years ago in Europe, most of the population was illiterate and weddings were announced by criers who walked through the streets bellowing the news. Much later the nobility and wealthy began to hire monks to scribe their invitations. In the 1600s, metal-plate engraving was developed and more people could afford to have their invitations printed and distributed.

Simple Invitation

This elegant bridal shower invitation takes only minutes to create. Begin with a premade lavender card. Print the invitation text onto white cardstock, trim it and adhere it to the inside of the card. Embellish with a patterned tag, ribbon and charms.

Jessie Baldwin

Personalized Thank-Yous

Create personalized thank-yous using ATCs (artist trading cards). These little cards are the size of baseball cards, and like baseball cards, artists trade them as personal calling cards. The format also makes great little keepsake thank-yous. Stamp, scribble and embellish your cards so they reflect your taste and personality.

Jessie Baldwin

Heritage Pages to Commemorate

Immortalize the past with vintage layouts

Extra! Extra! Look at the headlines! Historical news has been made throughout the centuries. Newspapers have documented war efforts, the lives of those back home, love and romance, sports and much more.

Like newspapers, scrapbook pages record the events and personalities of important people—our friends, neighbors and family members. The scrapbook pages we create today will be the heritage pages of tomorrow. Our descendents will learn about our lives and times by reading the information we share on our scrapbook art. The photos will give them insights into the world we lived in "way back then."

It is the lucky person who receives a gift of old family photos from a great-grandparent and an even luckier one who opens up an old suitcase stored in the attic for years only to find a treasure trove of memorabilia. If you have inherited these gifts from your ancestors, they are yours in trust. You have a responsibility to your descendents to preserve them in the highest quality and safest place possible—a scrapbook.

A YOUNG GIRL'S LIFE ABOUT TO BE INDELIBLY CHANGED

TELEGRAM

Nama was about 9 years old and the year was 1929 when this photo was taken. Little did she know that in a few short years the Great Depression would change her life forever.

Kathryn Balint

 To forget one's ancestors is to be a brook without a source, a tree without a root.

Chinese proverb

The Headlines Tell the Story

Throughout the centuries important events have been recorded in black-and-white and read all over

In towns and cities across America you could count on one thing: If an event was important, it made headline news. During wartime, papers churned out page after page of battle results and the lives of men and women in uniform. Scrapbooking photos of those in the military honors their service and holds their bravery up as a standard for their descendents.

Carolyn Cleveland

USO

The year was 1945 and WWII was raging. Women were contributing to the war effort in a number of ways—recycling, taking over the jobs of men who were serving, and entertaining the troops. This patriotic page includes patterned papers, tags, ribbons, stickers and a special piece of memorabilia.

"
I have always been fascinated by genealogy; even as a child...I started putting together my family tree in my early 20s so this information would not be lost...Then when scrapbooking became popular, it seemed like the perfect way to continue that effort.

Carolyn Cleveland
"

Teresa Bean

The Officers Club

Friendships remain strong among our servicemen. It's 1953 and these officers had a place to get together and tell stories. Their ebullient photo is scrapbooked elegantly on distressed patterned papers. Page turns, brads and alphabet buttons are as understated as the gentlemen's suits.

Q+a

Do you have any advice for cropping heritage photos?

STOP! PUT DOWN THOSE SCISSORS AND STEP AWAY FROM THE HERITAGE PHOTOS! Cropping heritage photos is like cutting a one-of-a-kind diamond: best not to be tried. One little slip of the scissors and the photo is ruined forever. For this reason, it is better to make copies of heritage photos. Scrapbook the copies (these you can crop to your heart's content) and safely store the originals.

Business News

While our brave young men and women serve their country, life on the home front moves forward. No matter what the decade, technology changes and businesses thrive. Scrapbook heritage photos to recall the daily lives and events of those who lived down the block and around the corner.

Fill 'er Up

This splendid montage of images and embellishments shows times when prices at the pump were a lot less strain on the ol' pocketbook. The artist's husband, brother and mother are shown in the photo standing in front of a family-owned gas station. Ribbon, washers, metal rings, chipboard stencil letters and patterned papers set the stage for the photo.

Kathryn Balint

ASKING YOUR ELDERS

Don't allow the opportunity to record information about your older family members to slip by. Make time to visit, and take along either a tape recorder or a notebook. Ask:

- Where did you grow up? What was your town/ neighborhood like?

- Did you have siblings? How many and what were they like? Who were you closest to and why?

- What did you most like to do when you were young? Did you play sports? Were you into music?

- What do you remember as your happiest time as a child? What was the most difficult time?

- What was your favorite dish as a child? Who made it for you and how often did you get it?

- What was your favorite toy? Where did it come from? What happened to it?

- How were the schools you attended the same and how were they different from schools today?

- Did you have a best friend? Tell me about the adventures you had! Did you ever get in trouble together?

- As a teen, how did you spend your hours after school? Did you have a girlfriend/boyfriend? What made you crazy about her/him?

- Did you go to college? Where? What did you study? Why did you choose your profession? If you could do it all over again, what would you do professionally?

- Where did you meet your spouse? What made you fall in love? What was your wedding like?

- Tell me about the birth of your children. Describe their personalities as they grew.

- If you could share one thought with your great-great-great-great-grandchildren, what would it be?

Family Tender Moments

Small family-owned stores continue to thrive. When a husband and wife truly enjoy being with each other, it is obvious to those around them. This photo captures a couple content with both their marriage and their circumstances. The image is scrapbooked on distressed patterned papers that have been crumpled and ripped. Distressed-effect tags hold both the page title and journaling. Chipboard squares with stamped letters creatively contribute to the layout.

Amanda Barras

> *It was a typical day in a small East Texas town where nothing much was going on. But, my mother decided to haphazardly snap a photo of my grandparents in their country store. And though it was an ordinary day, not unlike any other, the grin on my grandmother's face tells a story of an enchanted simpler life.*

Amanda Barras

Fashion and Trends

Hemlines this year are dropping. Sleeves are three-quarter length. Collars are lacy. Predictions by fashion experts is that next year's fashions will be...just the opposite! We follow fashion with as much interest today as did our ancestors before us. Scrapbook photos that show the clothing of the time on pages that tie attire to those who wear it.

My Grandma Roseanne

A stamped background supports a stamped and stitched title strip on this elegant page. Delicately dyed flowers, tiny heart brads, ribbon and lace embellish the layout. The jewel in the crown is the stickpin thrust through one of the flowers at the corner of the photo.

Missy Neal

PUTTING ON YOUR SLEUTH HAT

Oftentimes we inherit heritage photos but are provided with little or no information about the pictures. In these cases it is necessary to put on a Sherlock Holmes hat and search for clues about the photos' origins.

Look at the fashions worn by those in the photos. Hem lengths, fabrics, colors and styles change rapidly, and by comparing your photos with fashion history, you can narrow down the time frame in which the image was taken.

Study the background of your photos. Cars and technology change rapidly, and you may be able to identify models and makes that will help you identify when your photos were taken.

Look at the buildings seen in your photos. Not only does architecture change over time, neighborhoods grow. You can identify both a place and a time by exploring when certain buildings were constructed and where.

Share the images with friends, family members and even your local newspaper publisher. They may recognize those in the pictures.

The Swicegood Family

1908 equals fantastic fashions. The Swicegood family of North Carolina really knew how to dress. Photos of them are showcased on this wonderfully nostalgic spread backed with black cardstock and patterned paper. Each image is labeled with the name of the model. The title/jouraling block is held in place with rustic brads. Decorative brads and a fiber-wound tag complete the spread.

I don't have enough photos of my individual family members to create a full spread. What should I do?

Copy and enlarge the original photo and crop around the models in the copy. Use the cropped images on your corresponding page.

Susan Hubbs

Community Happenings

The events that take place right in our own backyards are always of interest. Both our concern and our curiosity make us want to know what is going on and who is doing what. Scrapbook events that are newsworthy on scrapbook pages that include school, ball games, hobbies and romance.

Patti Hozack

1958

Another class graduates to take their places in the world! Their photo is scrapbooked on a patterned paper background. Label tape, a tag bearing an inspirational quote and minimal embellishments keep the page simple but powerful. The tiny circular metal frame circles the featured class member—the artist's mother.

Not only did my heritage provide the solid roots to be a good person, but those roots subsequently gave way to wings that have allowed me to live my life to its fullest...

Patti Hozack

FLEA MARKET AND ANTIQUE STORE PAGE ADDITIONS

Heritage pages just call out to be embellished with vintage finds. Search your local flea markets, thrift stores and antique stores for special pieces to bring the flavors of the past to your scrapbook.

- Lace, trim, fabric and ribbon
- Lockets, necklaces and other pieces of inexpensive jewelry (you can often get a bargain-basement price on jewelry that is slightly damaged)
- Old postcards, magazines, books, maps, advertisements, photos and product packages

- Washers, screws and other pieces of rustic hardware
- Eyeglasses
- Bits of broken pottery, china or glass
- Silver baby spoons, silver snuff or pill boxes
- Old letters, telegrams and other pieces of correspondence

DON AND BAMBI HAD A SHORT BUT
SWEET FRIENDSHIP. HE AND GRANDMA
TOOK THE LITTLE FAWN IN WHEN HER
MOTHER DIED. SHE ONLY STAYED WITH
THEM FOR A FEW WEEKS BUT SHE
STAYED IN THEIR HEARTS FOREVER!

an unusual
FRIENDSHIP

Dana Zarling

> " *He and Grandma took the little fawn in when her mother died. She only stayed with them for a few weeks but she stayed in their hearts forever.* "
>
> Dana Zarling

An Unusual Friendship

Local boy befriends orphaned deer! This unusual friendship is scrapbooked on a page of earth-toned patterned papers. Eyelets, a decorative embellishment and a well-balanced title add to the layout.

First Date

Love may be in the air for local couple! Photos of this budding romance are scrapbooked on a page of red and earth-tone patterned papers. A slide mount holds the page title. Silk flowers and stitching decorate the layout. Journaling is slipped into the embellished envelope on the lower left portion of the page.

> " *I met Jim at work at New England Baptist Hospital. He was teaching the student nurses how to use oxygen in the operating room. I didn't like him at first. I thought he was arrogant. We went on our first date in 1950...* "
>
> Josephine McCauley (seen in the photo), as told to the artist

Julie McCauley

The "Junior" League

Children are our pride and joy, and it doesn't matter when they were born or lived. Parents love to dress them up in their finest attire and do their best to coax smiles from the cherubs for the camera. Scrapbook photos of your relatives as toddlers and youngsters. Include letters that they wrote in later years, or ask them to journal about the photos.

Marlene Clawser

Siblings

Chances are that these three little angels aren't always as sweetly compatible as they appear in this terrific heritage photo—or as spotless! But thanks to this lovely scrapbook page, they will always be remembered at their very best. The soft photo is matted directly on gentle patterned paper. Tiny photo corners and a filmy ribbon embellish the layout. Silver tags supply the most basic information about the models.

Grow

There is a special bond between siblings and family members that grow up sharing the same playpen. The roots of friendship that are established early on take hold and continue to flourish into adulthood. Scrapbook childhood photos on layouts that also feature "all grown up" pictures of the same children. These terrific images are displayed on a page ripe with a variety of different fonts and textures of lettering products. The large black title draws the eye while the fabric and resin lettering accents anchor both of the photos.

Wendy Chang

Carolyn Cleveland

Contentment

A peaceful moment in a young girl's life is captured in this lovely photo. The image is scrapbooked on a collaged background of ripped and rolled patterned papers. The embellishments, including the tags, ribbons and daisy die cuts, are edged in platinum ink. Buttons line the upper edge of the title. The journaling appears on a tag that is tucked behind a piece of patterned paper.

"

This is my favorite photo, taken in our back yard in 1952. I remember how prickly those lawn chairs were! But at that age...who cared? I wish my hair had stayed that color! I guess I already knew how to pose when the camera was around. But in my face I see the seriousness behind the slight smile. It's as if I knew the weight of the things to come in my life.

"

Carolyn Cleveland

Wedding and Society Pages

Love and marriage go together like a horse and carriage. We love romance and look forward to seeing our family and friends happily moving toward the altar. Because weddings are such a notable time in people's lives, they are usually well-photographed. Those cherished photos tend to be among the most carefully preserved of heritage photos. Give them a home on scrapbook pages that will keep them safe for generations to come.

Karen Robinson

Forever

Lacy patterned paper adds a romantic touch to this lovely heritage page. The photo of the bride and groom is matted on brown cardstock before being mounted on top of the lacy and stitched floral papers. A rub-on word forms the title. The decorative journaling tag is created with lacy ribbon, an eyelet phrase plaque, flowers and patterned paper. Decorative brads and a molding strip complete the layout.

Mr. & Mrs.

Vows are recited by local sweethearts. This black-and-white photo of a bride and groom in post-WWII years is scrapbooked on inked blocks of beautiful patterned paper. A green paper border strip resembling a ribbon is punched with a tiny leaf design. Rub-on letters add journaling to the border. The sticker title adds a graceful sweep across the lower portion of the page.

Linda Beeson

Wedding Day

A beautifully embossed title is the focal point for this simple but effective wedding spread. The ornate letters are brushed with pink ink and matted before being mounted to the pale green cardstock strip. Embossed white paper and floral paper form the background for the two wedding images. The wedding announcement (faux) is printed on vellum and decorated with pearl stick pins. A ribbon-tied pin serves as an exclamation point at the end of the page title.

Chester and Ella Boweman
and
Theodore and Florence Meyer
invite you to celebrate
the marriage of their children

Dolores Marie
and
Gerald Riley
on
Saturday, September 28, 1957
at
St. John's Evangelical Church
Chapline Street, Wheeling, WV

Karen Robinson, Photo: Theo Meyer

+Q
a

My family kept absolutely no memorabilia! I'd like to include some on my pages and feel so sad that it is no longer around. Any suggestions?

Once gone, memorabilia is truly gone, but you can create faux memorabilia (such as the wedding announcement on the spread above). Put down the facts, as best you know them, on a piece of vellum in a format that might very well have been used all those years ago.

Add More JOY

Heritage Keepsakes

Keep your memories rooted and close with timeless memory crafts

Heritage photos are particularly precious because they are rare and irreplaceable. Preserving and displaying vintage pictures is a way of honoring those who led the way. However, scrapbooking these special images is not the only way to preserve the photos. Consider using them to create beautiful memory art. These projects are a delight to own and also make wonderful gifts.

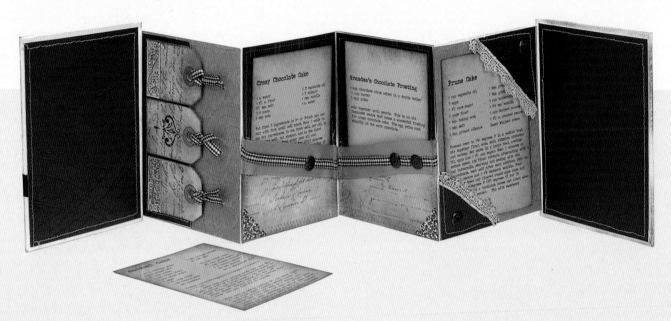

Samantha Walker

Recipe Book

Family recipes are a superb theme for heritage art. The recipes remind you of your loved ones and keep them alive with each recurrent preparation. This accordion card holds a grandmother's favorite cake recipes. Each recipe is printed on a laminated tag that can be removed for cooking reference. The laminated surface allows the tag to be cleaned after being used, if necessary.

A Pocket Full of Memories

This pocket album is ingeniously created with cone coffee filters which allow tags and other pieces of flat memorabilia to be slipped inside the open ends. (Be sure to treat the filters with acid-neutralizing spray before using.) A booklet cover is cut from patterned paper in the same shape as the filters. Two eyelets, set in the narrow portion of the filter booklet, are laced with ribbon to bind the album.

Becky Thackston

A Box of Love

This memory box holds dimensional memorabilia that is too bulky or heavy to fit inside a scrapbook. To create the box, begin with a plain photo box. Cover it with a large sheet of decorative paper. Ink the edges to give the box an aged look. Add green paper and stickers. Stamp fish designs onto paper and cut them out before adhering them onto the box. Complete the memory box with a copy of a vintage photo.

Samantha Walker

Winning Sports Pages

Scrapbook the success of today's athletes

It's Saturday or Sunday. Time to pack up those balls, bats, goggles, sticks, pucks and other equipment and take off to your favorite sports facility. If you aren't the one who is planning on chasing a ball, plowing through water, galloping around an arena or otherwise exerting herself, you will undoubtedly be cheering your head off and taking photos.

Sports entertain, but they also build bodies, character and relationships. Introducing a child to sports early in life is a good way to plant the seeds of a physically active lifestyle that will result in lifelong benefits. Photographing the sporting activities of children, family and friends demonstrates your respect for their efforts. Win or lose, the scrapbook pages you create with these photos show your pride and that you feel your athlete is a winner.

Today's sports-themed scrapbooking product is so extensive that you may find yourself running up and down the aisles of your local craft or hobby store excitedly looking for just the right buy. (Think of the calories that can be burned and the leg muscles we can build just shopping!) But don't rely on product alone for great sports pages. Include a piece of your heart in the journaling.

Now....on your mark, get set, GO have fun scrapbooking your very best sports photos!

GRAND SLAM

Lisa Dorsey

Champions aren't made in the gyms. Champions are made from
something they have deep inside them – a desire, a dream, a vision.
Muhammad Ali

Sports Offer a Bag Full of Benefits

Athletes reap a locker full of benefits, both physical and emotional

In this ever-changing world it's important to be able to stay balanced and keep your feet underneath you. Athletes master the challenge by focusing their eyes on the horizon. While stretching their skills—as well as their bodies—they are able to stay flexible, injury-free and in competitive shape.

Missy Crowell

Grace

Every successful gymnast starts training early, developing dedication and determination at a young age. Black-and-white photos featured on a stamped background of peachy cardstock show that this little girl has what it takes. Patterned papers, photo mats and edges and other elements are painted and inked for dimension.

LET'S TALK REAL FLEXIBILITY!

Contortionists take the art of flexibility to the extreme. Because they seem to be able to accomplish what no human body seems capable of performing, many myths have sprung up explaining "how" these feats of stretching are possible. Here are a few:

Myth #1: "Double-jointed" people have extra joints. **Debunked:** All people have the same number of joints but some are able to stretch them to allow hyper movement.

Myth #2: Contortionists dislocate their joints in order to bend so far. **Debunked:** While some contortionists can dislocate their

joints, most do not do so because it causes instability and can injure the athlete.

Myth #3: Contortionists apply snake oil to their joints or drink flexibility enhancing potions. **Debunked:** Flexibility is the result of genetics and intense physical training.

Myth #4: If one joint is exceedingly flexible, most of the joints will be the same. **Debunked:** Joint flexibility varies. A contortionist specializes in "tricks" based largely on which of his joints is most flexible.

Sk8er Boi

Skateboarding is, like, gnarly man! Just ask this kid. He's doing the bowls and grinding up a storm. Photos of his day at the skate park are featured on blue cardstock and patterned papers. A truly fantastic title composed of chipboard letters, tags, ribbons, staples, stickers and more defines the creative chaos of the layout. Journaling is hidden under the upper right photo on the left page.

This is the little boy that we were told might be autistic or have a brain tumor! Not hardly. I can't believe how good you are on a skateboard! This was only your 3rd time and you are already on the quarter pipe! I can only imagine how good you'll be in a few short years! I never lost faith in you all those years ago. So keep your faith too, baby!

Felicia Krelwitz

Felicia Krelwitz

Sports Improve Hand/Eye Coordination

Ever swung three times at a fly or mosquito and struck out? Then you may want to work on your hand/eye coordination. Sports are the perfect way to develop the skill. Many ball-and-stick sports offer intense practice, but archery, pingpong, golf and other activities can train your brain and hands to work in better synchrony.

Martha Walpole

A Keeper's Goal

Being a goalie is a lot like being a duck in a shooting booth with those balls being lobbed at you. But good goalies love the challenge of preventing balls from passing into the net. Photos of this athlete make it clear that she's got the temperament for the job. A clever title, tags journaled with rub-ons and the message displayed on the patterned paper reinforce that fact. Ribbons, a small "win" brad and a swath of mesh complete the layout.

Sonia Viglianti

The Greatest Game Ever Played

A collection of golf photos is matted and mounted on textured cardstocks. Rub-on words and a stamped title join vellum journaling blocks. The golf ball embellishments are cut from white paper, inked and embossed using a stylus to create the pattern. The wonderful figure of the golfer is created using a stained-glass pattern.

Tamara Joyce-Wylie

Dad/Mark

This man is sharing more than his knowledge of baseball. He's sharing time and building a bond that will last. The photos of the positive experience are scrapbooked on patterned papers. Large chipboard title letters are decorated with a flutter of ribbon. A file folder holds the journaling.

I have never tried to influence Foster on what to call Mark; I have left it up to him to use whatever name he feels comfortable with. He calls Mark by his name when he talks to him, but when he talks about him to someone else, 'Mark' becomes 'my dad.'

Tamara Joyce-Wylie

FAMOUS SPORTS FAMILIES

When fathers share their love of sports with sons, anything can happen. Sometimes the bond (and talent) that is handed down is so strong, careers are launched. Here are a few famous examples:

• Calvin and Grant Hill: Calvin was a famous running back for the Dallas Cowboys. His son, Grant, is an all star basketball player.

• Archie and Peyton Manning: Both father and son made the NFL's Top 50 for passes attempted and completed. Peyton's younger brother Eli now also plays quarterback in the NFL.

• Lee and Richard Petty: A father and son team of champion race car drivers.

• Gordie and Mark Howe: Hockey is their game, and these two players are considered outstanding within the NHL.

Sports Develop Motor Skills and Social Skills

It's mastering those gross motor skills that makes it possible for us to wear our bodies comfortably. Once we learn to drive "the machine" (our body) we can put it through all kinds of wonderful paces including running, kicking and dancing. Most sports help develop control over large muscle groups so we can move with confidence through life.

Micheal Evon

Athlete

Body language tells the story in this spread. The focal photo of the soccer player throwing herself into her kick is riveting. The photos are scrapbooked on patterned paper. A stamped title and sticker embellishments join a poetic journaling block.

Ride Like the Wind

She's on the go and nobody's gonna stop this young equestrian. Photos of her competition are showcased on a background comprised of strips of patterned papers adhered to a green cardstock base. Chipboard letters form the title. Metal-rimmed tags adorned with ribbons bring an extra dose of fun to the layout. An additional tag holds an in-motion photo.

Shuri Orr

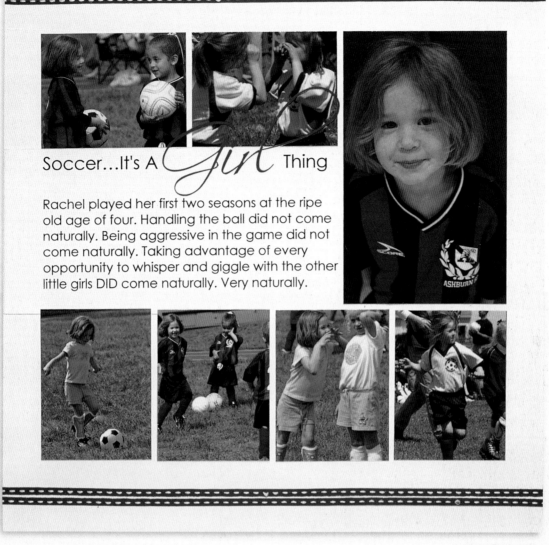

Soccer...It's A *Girl* Thing

Rachel played her first two seasons at the ripe old age of four. Handling the ball did not come naturally. Being aggressive in the game did not come naturally. Taking advantage of every opportunity to whisper and giggle with the other little girls DID come naturally. Very naturally.

Amy Dyckovsky

FAN ETIQUETTE

We adore our athletes and love supporting their efforts. but when our "support" turns the cheeks of our kiddo pink with embarrassment, it's time to rethink our cheering-section style. Here are some suggestions shared by veteran sideliners.

- Use the player's number rather than his name.
- Cheer for the "team" rather than an individual player. ("Way to go, guys!)
- Congratulate all who participated in a play including the scorer and those who assisted. ("Nice goal number 5! Great assist number 8!")
- Leave the coaching to the coach. Yell broad suggestions such as, "GO!" or "Score!" (Never call your player to the sidelines for a little "chat.")
- Never, ever yell something negative to your player or somebody else's.
- If you are having trouble with self-control, stick a lollipop in your mouth.

Soccer...It's a Girl Thing

"What do you mean I'm supposed to be kicking the ball? It didn't kick me first!" For this tiny soccer player the game is more about being social than serious about the competition. Photos of her "game face" are scrapbooked on a clean white textured cardstock background. Ribbon borders finish off the fun layout.

On Wheels, Wake or Foot, Sports Improve Fitness

Yep. It's all about heart—how hard you push it and how efficiently your system can circulate oxygen to those parts that need it. Pumping up that ol' heart rate burns calories and keeps the pump primed. Regular cardiovascular training should be a part of every athlete's workout.

Chris Douglas

Diggin' Dirt

Boys and speed go together, and as long as a helmet and appropriate protective clothing are included in the package, we can sit back and enjoy their feats. Photos of this dirt biker are scrapbooked on patterned papers and cardstock. A stamped title and screw heads as well as a journaling block are all that is needed to rev up the page.

Ashley Cantin

Mastering Wakeboarding

The focal photo on this spread is enough to make you catch your breath. It, and the other images, are scrapbooked on brown cardstock and slips of patterned papers. The journaling is found on an "evidence" card and embellished with buttons. More buttons, ribbon and a layered stamped title complete the layout.

Portrait of a Football Player

Six years old and hitting the gridiron like a pro—kinda—this young athlete is all about heart. Photos of his full-out efforts are scrapbooked on this graphic spread. A substantial journaling block, label tape, chipboard word plaques and a "champions" charm underscore the fact that this player has gone the full yard—and given it all his heart.

KARTER J~ YOU MIGHT NOT BE THE BIGGEST PLAYER ON THE TEAM, OR THE FASTEST. YOU DEFINITELY DON'T HAVE THE MOST EXPERIENCE, WHAT YOU HAVE IS SO MUCH MORE...HEART! A GREAT ATTITUDE. YOU GET OUT ON THAT PRACTICE FIELD EVERY DAY, IN THE GRUELING HEAT WITH YOUR FOOTBALL GEAR ON, READY TO GO! YOU RUN, YOU STRETCH, YOU DO DRILLS, ALL WITHOUT COMPLAINING OR CRYING...YOU JUST DO IT, BECAUSE THAT'S WHAT FOOTBALL PLAYERS DO! SOMETIMES YOU GET DISTRACTED (AFTER ALL, YOU ARE ONLY 6 YEARS OLD) BUT WHEN IT'S TIME TO HIT, YOU HIT HARD, YOU CAN TAKE A HIT TOO, AND YOU NEVER QUIT! NO FEAR~ THAT'S MY BOY! YOU PLAY FAIR, YOU CHEER ON YOUR TEAMMATES & YOU HAVE FUN! IF YOU ASK ME, THAT'S WHAT A FOOTBALL PLAYER IS~ HE'S YOU!

> "You run, you stretch, you do drill, all without complaining or crying... you just do it, because that's what football players do!"
>
> Lisa Kremer

Lisa Kremer

Q + a

What do I do if I can't find sports patterned paper that works with my particular concept?

Make your own! Paint the bottom of your shoe and step on a clean piece of dark cardstock to leave a footprint. Roll the threads of a ball across ink and then across your page. Ink up the treads of your bike tire and use it to stamp your layout. The possibilities are endless!

Sports Connect Effort and Accomplishment

Most wanna-be athletes know that practice isn't always fun. True, accomplished athletes learn to push past barriers of fatigue or boredom and focus on the end reward of their efforts. Whether measured by a trophy, a karate belt or a promotion, training is the difference between success and failure.

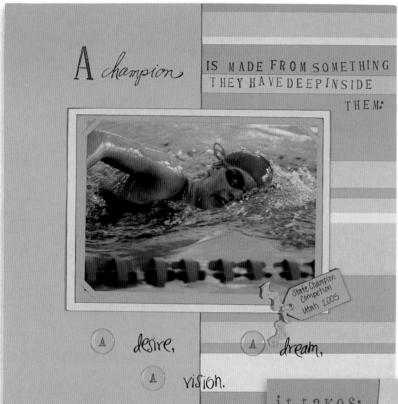

 There is no 'off-season' in swimming, just lots of practice year-round. I am constantly setting new goals and improving little by little. Obviously, this requires plenty of commitment to stick with such a vigorous program.

Natalie Rasmussen

It Takes Determination, Practice, Commitment

Winning takes drive, and this swimmer has it! Photos of her efforts are scrapbooked on brilliant-colored cardstock and patterned paper that perfectly match the water. Large stencil letters are used for the title. The journaling block is embellished with acrylic page pebbles that look like water droplets. Rickrack, brads and tags make this page a real contender.

Swimming isn't for wimps

It really does take a lot of determination, practice, and commitment. We have 5 a.m. practices in addition to our after-school practices, which last several hours. In the summertime we still have two practices daily. There is no "off-season" in swimming, just lots of practice year-round. I am constantly setting new goals and improving little by little. Obviously, this requires plenty of commitment to stick with such a vigorous program. During the regular season we have meets once a week. I'm always trying to achieve a new personal best time for each event I participate in. Weeks before the big meets, like region and state, we have taper. During taper we don't eat any sugar. We also have to be in bed by 10:30 and up by 6:30. The culmination of these efforts is realized on this one important day when I get to compete in the state championships. This is the day where I get to prove to myself and others just how far I have come and how I can be a winner. During this kind of competition it takes determination. It takes determination to be a little faster than I was before and hopefully just a little faster than the girl in the lane next to me.

Nicole Hansen, Photos: Kimball Rasmussen

Melanie Lawinger

Three Black Belt Buddies

Martial arts is as much about respect as it is kickin' tush, and these three boys would never be testing for their coveted black belts if they didn't understand that. Photos of the testing are scrapbooked on distressed-looking cardstocks. Fiber, eyelets and tags add to the spread.

Tough Cookie

A tough cookie doesn't crumble under pressure, and this tri-athlete has proven that she's worthy of the comparison. This digital layout includes extensive journaling that details the events of the competition.

Heidi Knight

Sports Inspire Confidence

Remember the little train that could? Despite the obstacles, that little engine dragged his line of cars up some of the steepest slopes in Picture-Book-Land. His mantra? "I think I can." Athletes develop a similar positive attitude and belief in their ability to meet and push past obstacles that might put off less-trained humans.

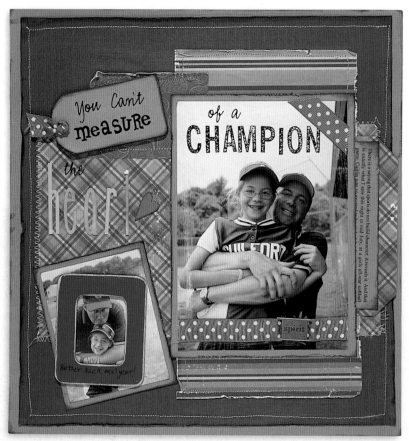

Linda Sobolewski

 There is a saying that sports do not build character, it reveals it. And that is exactly what I saw this night in mid-July at a girl's all-star-softball game... the other team scored over and over again. The whole team seemed to lose heart, everyone that is, except Caitlin!!!... Instead of giving up, like the other girls were doing, Caitlin was the only one who stepped it up a notch, giving it all her heart and soul.

Linda Sobolewski

The Heart of a Champion

Layered, distressed patterned papers are stitched to the background of this meaningful layout. The focal photo is embellished with a buckled belt while the support photo is matted and mounted beneath a journaled chipboard frame. An inked tag provides space for the first part of the title. Stickers and rub-ons are used to create the rest of the title.

THE POWER OF POSITIVE AFFIRMATION

Negative thinking can drag us down, making even simple tasks more difficult. But positive thinking, and most certainly the articulation of those thoughts, can have the opposite effect. Write your own affirmations to build confidence.

Keep your affirmation positive. Eliminate any negative words and include as many powerful action words as possible.

Make your affirmation speak to a specific problem or goal.

Use your affirmation often. Once written, begin and end your day with it.

Visualize the positive outcome you seek as you read your affirmation.

Request the help of a higher source, should you wish, in an invitation within your affirmation.

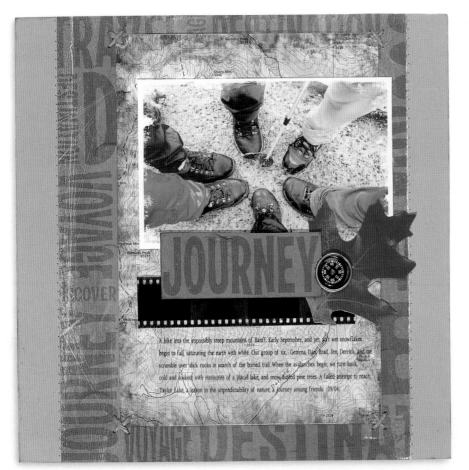

Journey

Nature is unpredictable, and those who decide to play in its back yard need to be prepared for anything. This dramatic photo illustrates the conditions that greeted these hikers, including mud and unexpected snow. The distressed patterned paper is stitched onto brown cardstock. A negative strip, leaf and tiny compass support the firm title.

Mary MacAskill

Last at Bat

The pressure is on and the photos of this young baseball player convey it. Mounted on a background that has been painted to capture that dirt-on-your-knees feeling, the photos are particularly intense. Stamped and chipboard lettering in the title completes the page.

The last game, the last at bat, the last swing of the season. It has been a season of ups and downs for Remington. He has struggled with batting. He gets up there and gives it his best but it was really hard for him to get a hit for some reason.

Syalynne Kramer

Syalynne Kramer

Sports Provide Youngsters With Role Models

We all need role models—somebody to look up to. From these heroes we gain hope. They provide us with a yardstick by which we can measure our own progress. Little athletes who are introduced to role models are lucky, and even luckier are those who find true mentors.

Keitha Fish

Tiny Tot Soccer

"I like it." "I don't like." "I like it." "I don't like it." It all depends on the day and the mood of the tiny athlete. This little gal found soccer both fun and—not so much. Photos are scrapbooked on a patriotic palette. Decorative ribbons, mini soccer balls and bottle caps embellish the page.

Batter Up

Batter, batter, batter SWING—or not. This little guy has yet to make up his mind. The compelling photo of him assessing the situation is scrapbooked on patterned papers designed especially for a layout such as this. For extra effect, they have been inked, as have the title and journaling blocks. The baseball paper clip is made by folding a brad around a paper clip.

Julie Richards

Batting Average

This lightweight is a heavy hitter! Photos of this softball player are scrapbooked simply on patterned papers and cardstocks. A stencil letter "B" and letter stickers form the title. The large numbers at the bottom of the layout are stamped. Journaling appears on a vertical vellum block.

> *Last year was the first year that she played softball. She had a hard time staying in the box and figured that if she just stood there long enough, she would get a walk. This year was totally different!*
>
> Chris Douglas

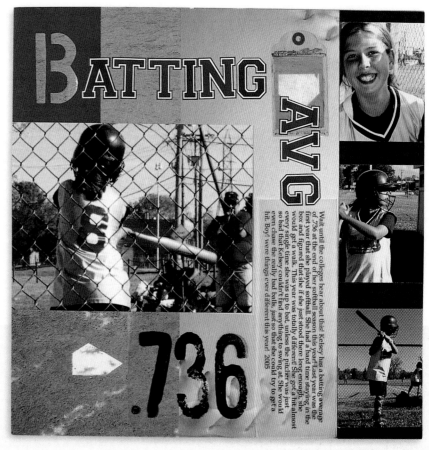

Chris Douglas

Baseball Camp MVP

Baseball is as American as apple pie, so scrapbooking this photo on red, white and blue patterned papers is a terrific choice. Stickers are used to create the title and they join photo turns and brads in embellishing the layout. Two solid pieces of corrugated cardboard supply a rustic, masculine feeling and dimension.

Keitha Fish

Sports Prepare Us to Face the Challenges of Life

Focus. Effort. Teamsmanship. Conditioning. Study. Practice. A good diet. Rest. All these are important for an athlete and all are equally important for living a successful life. Those who master the ABC's of athletics, are better prepared to be winners in the big world outside of the locker room and stadium. A winner is a winner, no matter what curveball he is thrown or where life takes him.

Chris Douglas

The ABCs of Softball

What better way to journal about a season of ball than to organize your thoughts around the alphabet. That's what this artist did, with terrific results. Photos and patterned papers make up the rest of the spread.

Wendy Malichio

Soccer Rocks

Soccer rocks and so does this terrific layout! There is no question about whether this athlete is confident and prepared to handle any challengers or challenges. The patterned papers, tags, frames and journaling all support the super black-and-white photo.

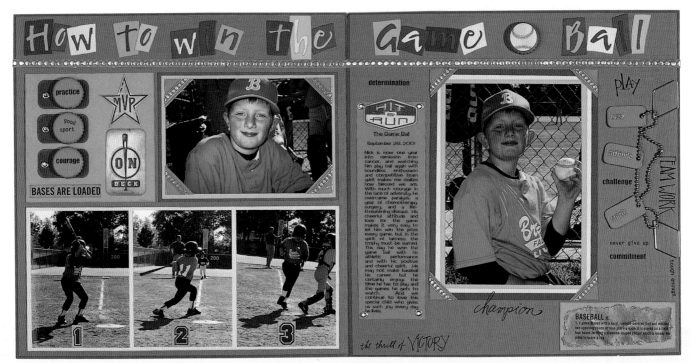

Nancy Walker

Game Ball

This young ball player knows all about winning. Having fought his way through surgery, paralysis and a year of chemotherapy, he is now in remission from his cancer and back playing the sport he loves. Photos of this survivor are double- and triple-matted on shades of teal and yellow. The photos, journaling block and other elements are mounted on a brown cardstock background. A sticker title pulls the color palette together. Embellishments include dog tags on a ball chain, bottle caps, brads, metal accent strips and metal photo corners.

> *Nick is now one year into remission from cancer, and watching him play ball again with boundless enthusiasm and competitive team spirt makes me realize how blessed we are...He may not make baseball his career, but he certainly enjoys the time he has to play and the games he gets to watch.*
>
> Nancy Walker

Doris Castle

Triumph

This young athlete has learned the rules, the skills and the meaning of both winning and losing. Her knowledge will serve her well. Photos are scrapbooked on a digitally created layout. All elements, including the embellishments, are created using computer software.

Scrapbooking with Found Objects

Seek "found objects" that can inexpensively and easily enhance sports scrapbook pages

When it comes to scrapbooking, sometimes your creativity needs to partake in the 7th-inning stretch. Get out of your craft room and open your eyes to the possibilities for creating unique sports-themed scrapbook pages using objects you have close at hand. No matter what sport you're scrapbooking, plenty of flat and lightweight mementos exist to help you create pages that really score!

Kathy Fesmire, Photos: Deb Cardin

Authentic Pigskin

Has your child made a super play? Save a piece of the game ball by scanning and printing the texture. The artist scanned the football her son kicked to achieve his first field goal. She enlarged the image and used it as a border, complete with authentic pigskin lacing, which was completed with a white shoelace. She used a smaller piece of the image on the journaling block.

Baseball Leather and Emblems

This page is the real deal. To showcase your child's baseball accomplishments, use the genuine leather casing of a baseball as well as an authentic embroidered emblem on your layout. To cut the skin from the baseball, carefully slice around a baseball. Cut the casing in half and flatten it before mounting it to your page. Add a few crisscross stitches with a leather strand to mimic the stitches of a baseball glove.

Kathy Fesmire, Photos: Deb Cardin

Kathy Fesmire

Team Schedules

When your child plays sports, family life tends to revolve around the demanding schedule of games and practices. The artist trimmed a schedule to use on this layout, which details her son's favorite part of the sport—the very demanding act of sitting sideline, enjoying a cold beverage. On the schedule, she used mini letter and number stickers to spell out the name of the soccer league and the date.

Index